GLASGOW
LAW JUNC.
CARSTAIRS
SYMINGTON
BEATTOCK
LOCKERBIE
GRETNA
CARLISLE
PENRITH
TEBAY
OXENHOLME
CARNFORTH
LANCASTER
PRESTON
WIGAN
WARRINGTON
CREWE
STAFFORD
LICHFIELD
TAMWORTH
NUNEATON
RUGBY
BLETCHLEY
TRING
WATFORD
HARROW
WEMBLEY
WILLESDEN JUNC
EUSTON
LONDON
Diagram of the Route
LONDON
to
GLASGOW

THE
CORONATION SCOT

The Streamline Era on the LMS

THE CORONATION SCOT

The Streamline Era on the LMS

Edward Talbot

Frontispiece: *No. 6221* Queen Elizabeth *climbing Shap with the down 'Coronation Scot' in 1937.*
M. W. Earley, courtesy Colour Rail

First Published 2002

ISBN 0-9542787-1-2

Printed by The Amadeus Press, Cleckheaton, West Yorkshire

Published by
Edward Talbot
32 Waterside Court, Gnosall, Stafford, ST20 0AR
et@steam.u-net.com

ACKNOWLEDGEMENTS

This book could not have been written without the co-operation of several organisations and the willing help of many friends and fellow enthusiasts. C. P. Atkins and John Edgington at the National Railway Museum went to great trouble to provide access to documents in the museum's archives. D. S. M. Barrie made available several items of memorabilia from his own collection as well as logs of runs which he had timed personally. Richard M. Casserley supplied much information on carriages, some of which appears in one of the appendixes. Harold Froggatt, a former fireman at Crewe North, related his experiences with the streamlined engines and carefully checked my account to ensure that they were accurately recorded, while Graham Roberts and Phil Edney supplied technical information on locomotive engineering and aerodynamics. Anthony J. East and Cliff Schoff in the United States went to great trouble to discover information about the 1939 tour of America. Dr Adrian H. Collyns, also in the United States, devoted much time and effort to unearthing photographs from American sources. Eric Russell was very helpful in looking up information and also supplied some of his own photographs. Roger Bell loaned some contemporary documents, as did Michael Brooks, as well as giving permission to use information from articles he had written. Yuko Ishibiki, Peter J. Stead and John Wardle gave invaluable help in many ways.

Graham Stacey of the Locomotive Club of Great Britain and Mike Smith of the Bournemouth Railway Circle were very helpful in arranging permission for pictures by K. A. C. R. Nunn and W. H. C. Kelland, the property of their respective societies, to be reproduced. W. A. Camwell and W. T. Stubbs kindly arranged for photographs by W. Leslie Good to be made available, Bruce Ellis kindly gave permission for photographs from the A. G. Ellis collection to be used, and Ron White of Colour Rail kindly loaned some photographs by M. W. Earley. Les Hanson went to great trouble to provide photographs he had taken himself. Michael Bentley supplied photographs from his own collection, including those by Leonard Hobdey and Harry Townley, and Paul B. Bromige read the text and made a number of invaluable suggestions. David Postle and Audie Baker of the Kidderminster Railway Museum made sure that prints of the best quality were produced from photographs in the museum's collection.

Finally Gerald Broom and Barry Freeman, the latter through the good offices of his wife Mary, made their superb paintings available for reproduction. I am most grateful to everyone for their help and extend to them my sincere thanks.

Edward Talbot
Stafford
September 2002

CONTENTS

		Page
Introduction		1
Chapter One	Concept and Construction	5
Chapter Two	High Speed and Regular Service	27
Chapter Three	'The Coronation Scot' in America	59
Chapter Four	Postscript	81
Appendix One	'Princess Coronation' Class Engine History Details	95
Appendix Two	Instructions to Signalmen for the Working of the 'Coronation Scot'	96
Appendix Three	Summary Details of 'Coronation Scot' Coaching Stock	98
Bibliography		98
Index		99

INTRODUCTION

When the directors of the London Midland & Scottish Railway Company decided to operate a high-speed passenger service between London and Glasgow they were responding to events and to the mood of the time rather than taking a lead. The immediate reason for their decision was probably the desire to compete with their rival East Coast company, the London & North Eastern Railway, but their choice of a streamlined train was very much in line with prevailing fashion both in Great Britain and abroad. More than most, 'The Coronation Scot' was a train that was the product of its time.

The streamline era of the 1930s was partly a reaction to the economic situation following the First World War. Immediately after the war there was at first a boom but it could not be sustained and recession followed. By the mid-1920s the situation was so serious that a General Strike occurred, but it made no difference and the slide into recession continued. In the United States of America the Wall Street Crash of 1929 finally marked the beginning of the depression, which then engulfed the whole of the industrialised world. It was well into the 1930s before the situation began to improve.

On the railways of Great Britain the First World War had taken its toll. The system had carried an unprecedented amount of traffic but maintenance had been severely limited and confined only to what was absolutely essential. Railway workshops had been turned over to war work, to a greater or lesser extent, and skilled men had been assigned to munitions production or recruited into the forces. Thus, permanent way, locomotives, rolling stock, signalling, plant and equipment of all kinds were generally in very run-down condition and in sad contrast with the generally excellent state of affairs which had prevailed before the war started.

This situation took some time to put right, since recovery was hampered by the recession, which depressed revenue and so restricted the availability of finance for repairs and renewals. It was well into the 1930s, when economic activity began to pick up, before the backlog of maintenance had been made good and schemes for improvements could be initiated. On the LMS the prime aim was to rationalise the vast system which had been created by the Grouping of 1923, so as to increase efficiency, to raise standards generally and to embark only on those schemes which would produce the greatest benefit. The large orders for new standard locomotives, to the design of W. A. Stanier, were only a part of these schemes.

Elsewhere in the world there was the same sort of reaction to the years of depression and an urge to cast off the drabness of the postwar years and move forward into a new, brighter, more exciting era. In America it was the age of the 'movies', of Hollywood, of glamour and of speed. Streamlining was all the rage, probably inspired by advances in aeroplane design, and came to be applied to trains, cars and even, in style at least, to houses and buildings.

The first country to introduce a high-speed streamlined passenger train offering superior service was

Plate 1: *No. 6224* Princess Alexandra *passes Oxheys with the down 'Coronation Scot' on 29th July 1937 . The driver has just reopened the regulator after slowing to run through Preston station. The contrast between the glamorous new train and the drabness of industrial Lancashire, doubtless still affected by the depression of the 1920s and 1930s, sums up well the impact of the train on the public. People stop whatever they have been doing to watch the train sweep by. Few of them are ever likely to have the resources and occasion to ride in it but it represents a glimpse of a more exciting way of life and hope of a better future. Similarly, the train had great impact on the morale of the LMS staff and was a source of great pride.*

E. R. Morten

Germany, which was also recovering from the aftermath of the First World War. In 1932 the German State Railways introduced the 'Flying Hamburger' between Berlin and Hamburg. The train was diesel-powered and as a result of its success a similar service was introduced between Berlin and Cologne. Plans existed for further expansion of these services and doubtless would have been carried out if the Second World War had not intervened.

In America the German lead was first followed by the Chicago Burlington & Quincy Rail Road, which introduced the first of its famous 'Zephyr' series of high-speed diesel trains, 'The Burlington Zephyr', between Chicago and Denver in 1934. Many other American railroads soon followed this example, some with diesel haulage and others with steam. Among the more famous were the Santa Fe's 'Super Chief', which was diesel-hauled, the Milwaukee Road's 'Hiawatha', for which a special series of 4-6-4 steam engines was built, capable of sustained speeds of over 100mph, and the New York Central's '20th Century Limited' and 'Empire State Express', which again were worked by special series of streamlined 'Hudson' 4-6-4s.

In Great Britain the directors of the London & North Eastern Railway were impressed by 'The Flying Hamburger' and wanted a similar service on the East Coast route between Kings Cross and Newcastle. Diesel power was considered, but the chief mechanical engineer, H. N. Gresley, took the view that such a train could be worked successfully by steam. Thus there came into service in 1935 the 'Silver Jubilee', which covered the 268 miles between London and Newcastle in four hours. The design of the train was sensational and quite unlike that of anything that had been seen before in the Britsh Isles. A matching silver-grey colour scheme was applied to both engines and carriages, in such a way that the whole train appeared to be a single unit. The effect was heightened by the styling of the streamlining, the wedge front of the locomotive being complemented by the beaver tail of the observation car at the rear. Nor was the change only external. The interior styling of the carriages and the accommodation and facilities they offered were equally revolutionary.

Thus 'The Silver Jubilee', with its striking and speedy new locomotives, was a great advance and set new standards of passenger-train speed. Previously, the fastest train in the British Isles had been 'The Cheltenham Flyer', which was scheduled to cover the 77 miles between Paddington and Swindon in 65 minutes at an average speed of 71mph. This train, however, was conventional in its design and was hauled by a conventional engine of the 'Castle' class, albeit one in excellent condition and specially prepared.

So the LMS, the largest of the 'Big Four' companies, found itself being left behind. It was well known that the LNER was planning to build on the success of 'The Silver Jubilee', and seeing its East Coast rival deriving such good publicity from its sensational new train, the LMS was spurred to do something similar. The result was 'The Coronation Scot'. In essence the idea was to provide a fast service between London and Glasgow with a train of striking design. The prime aim seems to have been to obtain publicity and match the LNER rather than just to provide a fast service as such.

To this end the LMS designers played their part to the full. The most noticeable features of the new engine and indeed of the new train were its colour scheme of coronation blue with silver stripes running the length of the train and the streamlined shape of the engine. These effectively gave the the train the necessary image, and combined with its performance on the road, enabled the company to mount a successful reply to the LNER. The new train also, incidentally, provided a boost to the morale of the LMS work force and a focus for pride in the company. This emerges clearly in conversation with former LMS employees.

In recent times several writers have criticised the streamlining of the engine on the grounds that it had little practical use, that it was only effective in reducing the power required at high speeds and that overall the additional costs it incurred were greater than the amount of coal it saved. Such views were not uttered at the time and conveniently ignore the whole point of the excercise, which was to compete with rival companies in the battle for publicity. Essentially the purpose of 'The Coronation Scot' was to capture the interest of the public and to enhance the image of the LMS. Lord Stamp himself was quite convinced of the effectiveness of the train as a means of achieving this end. Even if streamlining had produced no benefits whatsoever, it is inconceivable that the train could have been hauled by an unstreamlined engine, even one as impressive in appearance as the original 'Duchess'. If the LMS had attempted to match its rivals with a high speed service operated by such an engine, what would such critics have said then?

The introduction of luxury high-speed passenger services in the late 1930s seemed at the time to be just the beginning of a new period of development of such trains. Within a few years a network of similar services was likely to have come into existence. Though diesel traction was being tried abroad, it was still merely an interesting experiment rather than a serious threat to steam, which was perceived as having no serious rival. New more powerful engines were planned to work the extended services and would have been built if the Second World War had not intervened.

Though it was not realised at the time, however, the streamlined engines of the late 1930s were destined to represent the highest achievements of British steam locomotive engineering. The technical advances of the postwar period were not applied to producing performances superior to those which had occurred before the war, and certainly for many LMS enthusiasts the 'Coronation' class Pacifics remained unequalled in design, performance and style by any later variant or class. Similarly the train itself and the service it provided was never surpassed by the LMS or its successors with steam traction.

Plate 2: *The first three newly completed 'Princess Coronation' class engines posed for the offical photographer outside the Paint Shop at Crewe Works in May 1937. They all have coal in their tenders and so have probably been to Crewe North shed for coaling.*
Courtesy Dr Adrian H. Collyns

Chapter One
CONCEPT AND CONSTRUCTION

The proposal to introduce a new London-Glasgow service on a $6^1/_2$ hour schedule was first announced by the chairman, Sir Josiah Stamp, at the annual general meeting of the company on 26th February 1937. Much work had already been done to investigate the possibilities of operating such a high-speed service. On 16th November 1936 a test train weighing 225 tons tare was hauled from Euston to Glasgow in the record time of 5hr 53min by 'Princess Royal' class 4-6-2 locomotive No. 6201 *Princess Elizabeth.* It also set a new record of 122min for the 141 miles from Crewe to Carlisle, beating the time of 126min which had been achieved by the celebrated LNWR 'Jumbo' No. 790 *Hardwicke* during the 'Races to the North' in 1895. The following day No. 6201 returned from Glasgow to Euston with 255 tons, again setting a new record time of 5hr 44min.

This part of the preparations was very much in the public eye but much other less spectacular work had already been going on for some time. A new class of streamlined locomotives had been designed and was under construction at Crewe, while three sets of carriages were being prepared at Wolverton. Much work was also being carried out to improve the track and to make it suitable for sustained high-speed running.

The name of the new service, 'The Coronation Scot', was an excellent choice. It honoured the coronation of King George VI and Queen Elizabeth which took place on 15th May 1937 and so was topical, and it also extended the 'Scot' theme of the company's Anglo-Scottish named trains, 'The Royal Scot' and 'The Mid-day Scot'.

For similar reasons it was decided that the name of the first of the class of new engines should simply be *Coronation.* The idea was originally put forward in February 1936 when the Vice President, Sir Harold Hartley, suggested that one of the Pacifics should commemorate the coronation of King Edward VIII. He wished to perpetuate the name of the LNWR 'George the Fifth' class 4-4-0 which had been so named in honour of the coronation of King George V and Queen Mary in 1911 and carried a special nameplate surmounted by a crown. Hartley wanted this nameplate transferred to the new engine but Stanier rejected the idea as 'completely inappropriate for a revolutionary design of powerful, high speed streamlined locomotives'. In August 1936 Derby supplied a sketch of a nameplate in the 'Princess Royal' style but with a crown over it. Again Stanier rejected the idea. He already thought the nameplates used on the 'Princess Royals' were too insignificant on such large engines. Few would disagree.

By the end of 1936 it had been decided that the new engine should be streamlined and Stanier was seeking a metallurgist's report on a new metal reputed to have the appearance of 18 carat gold. This idea was soon dropped and Stanier then asked H. G. Ivatt at St Rollux for two panels to be prepared in genuine Caledonian Railway blue, one plain and the other with silver stripe. Although the colour was later officially described as 'light blue', its Caledonian origins seem beyond doubt.

On 18th January 1937 three schemes were put forward for the engine livery and nameplates. In all cases the latter was described as a 'symbolic wing' and in two of the three the engine had stripes consisting of chromium-covered stainless-steel bands. In the first design the crown was above the nameplate but it was felt that in that position it interfered with the stripes. In the second the crown was on the cab side, and the third was the same but without the bands. The crown was to be based on the St Edward crown with the individual jewels enamelled. At this time the Publicity Department still seems to have been unaware of the decision to use

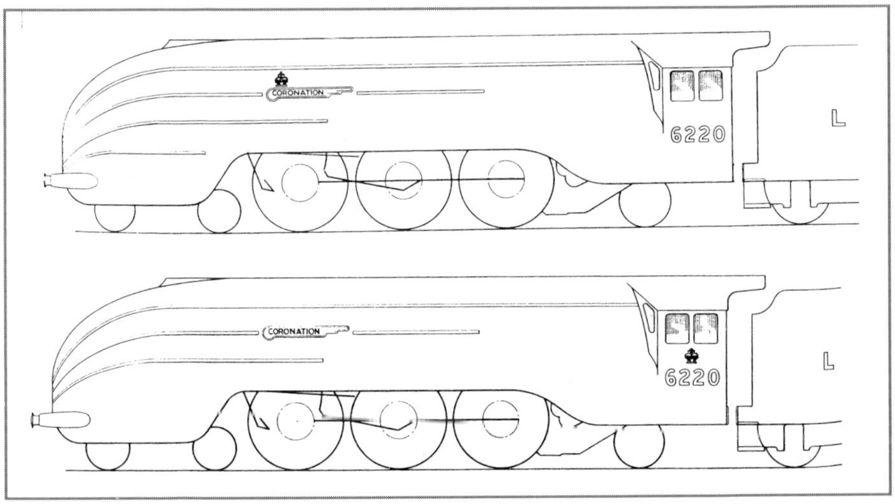

Figure 1: *The first two schemes for the streamlined engine with 'symbolic wing', crown and metal stripes.*
(Courtesy, Michael Brooks)

Plate 3: *General view inside the wind tunnel, showing models of* Coronation, *an aeroplane and a car.*
National Railway Museum

blue and silver and was talking of publicising the new train as the 'all-gold' route to Scotland.

Eventually all the wing designs were rejected in favour of a conventional straight plate with a crown placed above it. In April Stanier approved the design of crown, suggesting that it should be cored at the back and sprayed with silver. Similarly, the idea of metal bands on the engine was also rejected, the Paint Research Department producing a detailed specification setting out the various steps to be taken in painting an engine over a fifteen-day period.

When the new Pacific was completed, the LNWR engine lost its distinctive nameplates, to prevent the company having two engines with the same name at the same time, but only after it had featured in a film with the new engine. Early on Sunday morning, 13th June, all four lines were blocked between Llandudno Junction and Colwyn Bay, while No. 6220 with 'The Coronation Scot', the LNWR *Coronation* with the '1911 Coronation train' and the Liverpool & Manchester Railway *Lion* with the 1830 replica train ran side by side for the cameras. The name of the second engine of the class was *Queen Elizabeth* and the rest of the first batch of five engines were also named after female royal personages, following the theme of the 'Princess Royal' class.

Indeed the new streamlined engines were officially regarded merely as a development or adaptation of the 'Princess Royal' class for high-speed work. Initially at any rate that was how the original design was conceived, being referred to officially as the 'Princess Royal Coronation' class. As the design-work proceeded, however, the drawing office incoporated various improvements and so the final design differed in several important respects from that of the 'Princess Royals'. Certainly it was sufficiently different for the class to be regarded as a separate class in its own right.

Nevertheless in early official documents the class is referred to both as the 'Princess Royal Coronation' class and the 'Coronation Princess Royal' class. Eventually the name which came to be used officially by the company was the 'Princess Coronation' class. This name was used to refer to the whole class and continued to be so used even when all the engines in the class had lost their streamlining. Enginemen of course had their own nickname, 'Big Lizzies', to distinguish them from the 'Princess Royals', which were referred to as 'Lizzies'.

The term 'Duchess' class originated with the first five non-streamlined engines, which were all named after 'duchesses'. It is merely an enthusiast nickname that was applied at first only to those five engines but in recent years its use has widened to mean any of the non-streamlined engines and nowadays generally refers to the whole class. The term 'Coronation' class used in this book refers to the streamlined engines only, to distinguish them from the non-streamlined variant.

Wind Tunnel Research

In order to determine the most efficient shape for the new engine, the research department at Derby carried out a programme of 'streamlining experiments' which were described in a report dated 24th September 1937. Officially the purpose of the tests was 'to reduce air resistance on the engine as far as possible consistent with the requirement of the chief mechanical engineer to produce a practical machine'.

The experiments were conducted in the department's wind tunnel using a model of a 4-6-2 engine made to a scale of 1/24. The model was supported by thin steel wires above a flat plate representing the ground. When measurements of air resistance were being made, a model of a standard coach, built to the same scale, was mounted behind the engine. In most tests it was fixed to the ground plate but for some, such as those concerned with the effect of a cover over the tender, it was slung on wires in the same way and joined to the engine. The wires supporting the models were connected to sensitive balances outside the wind tunnel and so enabled the aerodynamic forces to be measured over a wide range of speeds up to 90ft per sec.

Two main groups of experiments were carried out, one to represent the condition of still air, so as to simulate the effects of head and favorable winds, the other to represent the effect of a side wind. In the first the model was placed parallel to or along the air stream; in the other it was placed with its longitudinal axis at an angle of 20° to the air stream.

Air resistance was measured first with the engine in its non-streamlined form and then in streamlined form. The shape of streamlining tested originally was designed according to known aerodynamic principles and best contemporary practice; but to enable the design to be developed the model engine was made so that the boiler and cab could be removed from the frame and replaced by a streamlined shape made of polished wood. Alternative forms of front end could be readily fitted to this wooden shape, as could various shapes and depths of side valances shrouding the wheels and cylinders, of covers for the cab and tender, and of screens or fairings for the undercarriage, axle-boxes and rear end of the tender. These experiments determined the most effective shape of streamlining and enabled the chief mechanical engineer to decide the shape and extent of fairing adopted in the actual engines.

As well as investigating the air resistance to the locomotive, experiments were also made to discover whether the driver's lookout from the cab would be obscured by exhaust from the chimney. In these tests the models were fixed on the ground plate and smoke from rags smouldering in a container was passed by piping to a passage in the engine boiler. It was arranged that the smoke would leave the chimney with a low efflux velocity relative to the speed of the locomotive through the air so as to simulate the condition of drifting. Smoke is more likely to obscure the cab in those conditions than when the engine is working with a powerful blast.

The streamlined forms were found to be superior to the conventional locomotive as regards smoke obscuration. Shapes having a backward-sloping flat front as in the LNER 'A4' class or having a channel recessed in the fairing ahead of the chimney as in some overseas engines had no advantage over *Coronation*.

To anticipate a possible service requirement, several different types of smoke deflectors were also designed and tested. They all succeeded in lifting the exhaust clear of the engine in a head-on wind and somewhat improved it in side winds but the most effective designs inevitably increased the air resistance of the engine. For that reason it was considered a valuable advantage of the *Coronation* shape that it was effective in lifting the exhaust clear of the cab and that as a result smoke deflectors would probably not be necessary in practice.

The tests established that four main features of the streamlining were important in reducing air resistance: rounding the front of the engine and making the whole external surface smooth, continuous and free from irregularities and projections; shrouding the wheels and motion with side valances; raking back the front of the cab where it joined the boiler casing; and covering the tender and extending its roof and sides to the rear, so as to reduce the pressure on the end of the first coach.

Altogether five different styles of front end were tested, including one which was similar to the 'A4'. The shape eventually adopted for *Coronation* gave the lowest air resistance of the series, about 2 per cent better than the 'A4' at 0° yaw and about 20 per cent better at 20° yaw. It was considered to be as good a shape aerodynamically as was likely to be achieved within the limitations of mechanical design.

Nevertheless, its air resistance considerably exceeded that of an 'ideal' locomotive tested during previous research. This work had established that the shrouding of wheels and motion reduces air resistance significantly (and implies, incidentally, that the removal of the valancing from the 'A4' class during the war to ease maintenance increased air resistance greatly). It was found that if the wheels are unshrouded, or partly unshrouded as in the case of *Coronation*, disc instead of spoked wheels reduce resistance in side winds considerably. Wheels of this type were never fitted to the 'Coronation' class but were used on some overseas engines. The New York Central 'Hudsons' employed on the 'Empire State Express', for instance, had boxpok

Table 1 - Air Resistance of *Coronation*

(i) Air resistance and horsepower absorbed at 0° yaw.
With the train travelling through still air, the train speed equals the 'resultant wind speed'.

Train speed (mph)	Air resistance (lb) Standard locomotive	Streamlined locomotive	Horsepower absorbed Standard locomotive	Streamlined locomotive
60	742	336	119	54
80	1318	598	281	128
100	2061	934	550	249

(ii) Air resistance and horsepower absorbed at 20° yaw.
The values for total air resistance are based on a model experiment which showed that the forward or tractive resistance due to a lateral force amounted to 1.45% of the lateral force. The values for horsepower relate to the special case of a side wind blowing at 35% of the train speed at 80° to the train direction; in these conditions the 'resultant wind speed' has the same speed as the train and is inclined at 20° to the length of the train. The official report uses the term 'resultant wind speed' but for clarity this has been replaced in the tables here by 'train speed', since in all cases in the report the two are equal.

Train speed (mph)	Speed of side wind (mph)	Longitudinal force (lb) Standard locomotive	Streamlined locomotive	Lateral force (lb) Standard locomotive	Streamlined locomotive
60	21	1180	590	2750	2920
80	28	2100	1045	4880	5190
100	35	3280	1630	7630	8110

Total Air Resistance

Train speed (mph)	Speed of side wind (mph)	Tractive force (lb) Standard locomotive	Streamlined locomotive	Horsepower absorbed (lb) Standard locomotive	Streamlined locomotive
60	21	1220	630	195	100
80	28	2170	1120	460	240
100	35	3390	1750	905	465

Table 2 Savings due to streamlining (based on 520 trips a year)

0° Yaw

Train speed (mph)	Air resistance (lb)	% of total train resistance	Horse-power	Coal/annum (tons)
60	406	6.1	65	187
80	720	8.0	153	441
100	1127	9.4	301	850

20° Yaw

Train speed (mph)	Air resistance (lb)	% of total train resistance	Horse-power	Coal/annum (tons)	Speed of side wind (mph)
60	590	5.4	94	272	21
80	1047	7.7	223	640	28
100	1638	8.6	438	1255	35

wheels, though whether the reduction of air resistance was a factor in their adoption is uncertain.

Streamlining the locomotive reduced air resistance by about 50 per cent, which corresponded to a reduction of about 7 per cent in the total resistance of 'The Coronation Scot' train. This reduction was greater during strong side winds and would have been consistently greater if overall train speeds had been increased. On the assumption that coal consumption was 1.9lb per indicated horse-power hour, the fuel saving on 'The Coronation Scot' schedule due to the reduced power output required because of streamlining was calculated to be about 10cwt per trip of 401 miles. This was equivalent to between £200 and £300 per annum, depending on the speed and direction of the natural winds. Against this saving had to be offset the initial cost of the streamlining and any increases in running and maintenance costs attributable to it.

The Train Completed

Preparations for the introduction of the new service began to show tangible results in the spring of 1937. The first of the new engines was completed at Crewe Works and the event was fully exploited by the publicity department. A train of the new stock was brought to Crewe from Wolverton where it had been prepared and both engine and train were displayed in the works yard for the benefit of the press on Tuesday 26th May. Before proceeding to the works, the press party was welcomed at a special lunch in the Crewe Arms Hotel by Mr W. A. Stanier himself. The inspection of the new train then followed under the guidance of Mr F. A. Lemon, the works superintendent.

To mark the occasion, *The Railway Gazette* produced a special issue describing the new engines and the train in detail, and lavishly illustrated with both photographs and drawings. It began by saying:

> 'The attractiveness of the 6½-hour timing between Euston and Glasgow will be increased by the fact that the journey will be made in new and very comfortably appointed trains hauled by streamlined locomotives built specially for the service. The distance by the LMSR route is 401½ miles, and the actual running time, allowing for a 5min service stop at Carlisle, is 385min, an average speed of 62.6mph. The style of painting adopted, namely Coronation blue with silver striping, gives a most striking outward appearance to the new locomotives and trains, and the use of chromium-plated fittings, and the new pattern electric lighting and upholstery designs in the coaches, combine to effect a *tout ensemble* upon which it would be very difficult to improve.'

The Engine and Train in Detail

The special issue of *The Railway Gazette* contained a full description of the construction of the engine and carriages. It is reproduced below:

The Engine

The 'Coronation' class Pacifics developed for the new service are essentially an improved version of the 'Princess Royal' class. Apart from the streamlining and many other detail features, the main improvements concern the boiler and the cylinders. To provide an adequate reserve of power, the capacity of the boiler to produce steam has been greatly enhanced by considerably enlarging the grate area, firebox, heating surface and superheater. So as to make the engine more suitable for sustained high-speed running, the cylinders are designed to make better use of the steam and are slightly enlarged, with a new arrangement of valve gear. Instead of four separate sets of valve gear, one for each cylinder, two sets of outside gear drive the inside valves through rocking levers. These levers are pivoted on needle roller bearings, which are used in the valve motion generally. The piston valves are of lightweight design and are fitted with six narrow rings to ensure steamtightness.

The following table contains comparative details of the last batch of 'Princess Royal' class Pacifics and the first batch of the 'Coronation' class:

	'Princess Royal' Nos. 6203-6212	'Coronation' Nos. 6220-6224
Cylinders	16¼ in by 28in	16½ in by 28in
Valve gear	4 sets Walschaert	2 sets Walschaert
Valve travel	7¼ in	7 1/32 in
Coupled wheels	6ft 6in	6ft 9in
Boiler		
Working pressure	250lb psi	250lb psi
Firebox heating surface	217sq ft	230sq ft
Tube heating surface	2097sq ft	2577sq ft
Total	2314sq ft	2807sq ft
Superheater	653sq ft	856sq ft
Combined heating surface	2967sq ft	3663sq ft
Grate area	45sq ft	50sq ft
Tractive effort at 85% boiler pressure	40,300lb	40,000lb

Boiler and Firebox Details

The boiler shell is constructed of nickel steel and the inner firebox of copper. The firebox stays are generally of steel, but the outer and top few rows, and the throat plate stays, are of Monel metal. The firebox is extended into the barrel to form a combustion chamber so as to allow combustion to be completed before the gases enter the tubes. The large flues are screwed into the firebox before being expanded. The firedoor is of the sliding type, carefully designed to direct the incoming secondary air down on to the fire.

A Davies & Metcalfe exhaust steam injector with 13mm cones is fitted on the fireman's side and a live steam injector with 13mm cones on the left-hand or driver's side; both injectors are of the flooded type. They deliver water to the boiler through top feed clack valves which discharge into trays within the steam space, wherein any gases contained in the water are enabled to be released; the de-aerated water is finally discharged through pipes below the water level. The superheater has 40 flue tubes, all containing triple elements each of 1in outside diameter; thus the steam passing to the cylinders is split up into 120 paths. The regulator, of the grid type, is located in the steam dome. Baffle plates are provided beneath the dome to prevent water from lifting and entering the steam pipe. Particular care has been taken in the design of the steam and exhaust pipes in the smokebox to keep the floor of the smokebox free of obstructions so as to facilitate the removal of ashes.

The boiler is fitted with four pop safety valves of 2½in diameter. Steam for the various fittings is taken from a manifold on the top of the firebox backplate in the cab. The fittings are of the company's standard type, though the carriage warming reducing valve is of increased capacity to deal adequately with long trains. A sand gun is fitted to enable the tubes to be cleaned during a run.

Frames, Cylinders and Motion

The main frames are 1⅛ in thick and are made of high tensile steel. At each side at the hind end two separate frame plates are spliced to the main frame and carried through to the hind buffer beam. The outer frames are splayed outwards and the inner frames inwards to take the side bearers for the trailing two-wheeled truck. The four cylinders of 16½ in diameter by 28in stroke have piston valves of 9in diameter with a maximum travel of 7 1/32 in. There are two sets of Walschaert gear outside the frames, driving the outside piston valves direct and the inside ones by means of rocking levers. The whole arrangement has been specially designed to allow the removal of both sets of valves for examination with the minimum amount of trouble. The valve motion is provided with Hoffmann needle bearings, except for the big ends of the eccentric rods which are fitted with SKF self-aligning ball bearings. The lubrication of the needle bearings is by grease gun.

The exhaust passages in the cylinders are carefully designed to give free exit to the steam without providing an excessive volume which would act as a reservoir. The exhausts from the inside cylinders and from the two outside cylinders are combined in the saddle casting, so that the blastpipe is a simple straight pipe. The piston valves are designed for lightness and are fitted with six narrow rings to ensure steam tightness. The pistons are of the box type, screwed on to the piston rods, and are provided with three narrow rings. Mechanical lubrication is provided for the cylinders, and the oil to the piston valve liners is atomised by being mixed with a jet of saturated steam taken from an independent supply on the boiler, so that atomised oil is supplied continuously while the engine is running, whether the regulator is open or shut. In addition to the feeds to each of the piston valve liners there are feeds to each piston packing and two feeds to each cylinder barrel, one at the top and one at the bottom.

The crossheads are of the two-bar type and are steel castings with bronze slippers, the surfaces which make contact being white-metalled. The gudgeon pin is prevented from turning in the crosshead by two keys and is secured by a split cone and nut. The couplings and connecting rods are of Vibrac steel and are designed to withstand the inertia stresses due to high speeds. The tyres are secured by the Gibson ring type of fastening, and the wheel rims are of triangular section. The balance weights are such that 50 per cent of the reciprocating weights are balanced, equally divided between the coupled wheels. The whole of the revolving parts are balanced in each wheel.

Axles, Wheels and Springing

The axleboxes are steel castings with pressed-in brasses completely lined with white metal on the bearing surface. There are no oil grooves in the crown of the box to disturb the continuity of the oil film, but the oil from the mechanical lubricator is introduced through a row of holes on the horizontal centre line of the axle. Hollow axles are used throughout, the internal diameters being 4½in for the coupled wheels, 3in for the trailing wheels and 2in for the leading bogie. In addition to mechanical lubrication, every axlebox underkeep is fitted with an efficient oil pad arranged to be easily withdrawn for examination. A dust shield is also provided on the inside faces of the intermediate and trailing coupled axleboxes. The supply of oil from the mechanical lubricator is taken through a spring-loaded back-pressure valve fixed at the top of the axlebox, the function of which is to keep the oil pipes full of oil while the engine is standing, so that delivery to the journals begins immediately the engine moves. The sides of the axleboxes are fitted with bronze slippers, making contact with the faces of the axlebox guides.

Plate 4: *Head-on view of the front end showing the four cylinders, the steam chests and the upper framing.*
Railway Gazette

Plate 5: *General view of the main frames in No 10 Erecting Shop at Crewe Works, taken during an enthusiast tour on 18th April 1937.*
L. Hanson

Plate 6: *The main frames from the rear end.* Railway Gazette

Plate 7: *The main frames from above.* Railway Gazette

Plate 8: *The boiler mounted in the frames.* Railway Gazette

Plate 9: *The boiler ready for mounting in the frames.* Railway Gazette

Side bolsters transmit the load from the main frames to the leading bogie. The bearing springs are of the inverted laminate type with screw adjustment. The trailing two-wheeled truck is of the Bissel type, and the bogie arm is anchored to the engine cross stretcher immediately in front of the firebox throat plate. As in the case of the leading bogie, the weight from the main frames is taken through side bolsters.

All the laminated bearing springs for the engine and tender are made of silico-manganese steel; the plates are of ribbed section with the cotter type of fixing in the buckle. The spring links are screwed to permit of adjustment. Rubber damper springs are also provided between the spring link heads and the frame brackets for the coupled wheels. A steam brake is provided, actuating brake blocks arranged at the front of the three pairs of coupled wheels. The brake gear is compensated to give equal pressure on each brake block. The driver's brake valve controls proportionately the application of the steam brake on the engine and the vacuum brake on the train. Separate steam valves are used for controlling the steam to the large and small ejectors. A vacuum pump, driven from one of the crossheads, is also provided.

Other Engine Details

The cab has double sliding windows fitted on both sides. On the outside of the windows are small glass screens, which can be turned into position when the enginemen are looking out of the cab, to deflect the draught. There is a hinged window giving ample area for lookout on each side in the front cab-plate. Tip-up seats are provided on both sides of the cab, and gangway doors are fitted between the engine cab and tender panel plates. Steam sanding is applied in front of the leading and middle coupled wheels for running in a forward direction and behind the middle coupled wheels for running backwards. Oil gun lubrication is used on certain parts such as the brake gear, spring gear and reversing gear in the cab.

Tender Details

The tender carries 10 tons of coal and 4000 gallons of water and is modified in shape to match the streamlining of the engine and the shape of the coaches. The coal pusher consists of a steam cylinder mounted on the back of the tender. It is designed to push the coal forward towards the fireman's shovel and can thereby save considerable manual effort at the end of a run. A door gives access to the coal bunker from the footplate, and on the fireman's side a long receptacle is provided to carry the fire-irons. The tender is provided with water pick-up gear of the company's standard type; a deflector is fitted in front of the scoop to reduce wastage of water. Oil gun lubrication is also used for such items as the handbrake and water pick-up handles.

Contractors

The following firms supplied equipment for the engines:

Main frame plates and boiler plates	Colvilles Limited
Vibrac steel coupling and connecting rods	English Steel Corporation Limited
Copper firebox plates	ICI Metals Limited Thomas Bolton & Sons Ltd
Monel metal firebox plates	H. Wiggin & Co Ltd
Superheater elements	The Superheater Co Ltd

The Carriages

The general construction of the coaches follows LMS standard practice, the body sides, ends and roof being covered with steel panels finishing flush with the windows. The exterior painting is carried out in blue, with four bands of silver running the full length of the train between the windows on the carriages and continuing at the same level on the engine to finish in a 'V' point on the front of the smokebox streamlining. The car numbers and lettering are in plain silver block characters and the exterior fittings such as door and commode handles are finished in chromium plate. The cars are carried on steel underframes with specially designed bogies.

All vehicles except the kitchen cars are equipped with pressure heating and ventilation of the Thermo Reg type, separate hot and cold systems being provided so as to ensure the maximum range of temperature control. Air is delivered through nozzles situated above the windows in the vestibule cars and above the windows and doors in the corridor cars. The nozzles can be adjusted by the passengers to give any desired temperature. In addition, the usual steam heaters are provided under the seats in every saloon and compartment. Double sliding lights, which can be adjusted either to extract air or admit it, are fitted above every window.

Interior Decoration and Lighting

The interior decoration is carried out on modern lines, so as to obtain a flush finish throughout the trains, the body-side walls, cornice

Plate 10: *The engine wheeled and with the framework supporting the streamlined casing fitted, 7th May 1937. At this stage, before the outer casing hides it, the chimney is seen to be a stovepipe.* National Railway Museum

Plate 11: *Rear view of the engine at a slightly more advanced stage three days later on 10th May 1937.* National Railway Museum

Plate 12: *The cab on completion but before the fitting of the floor.*
Railway Gazette

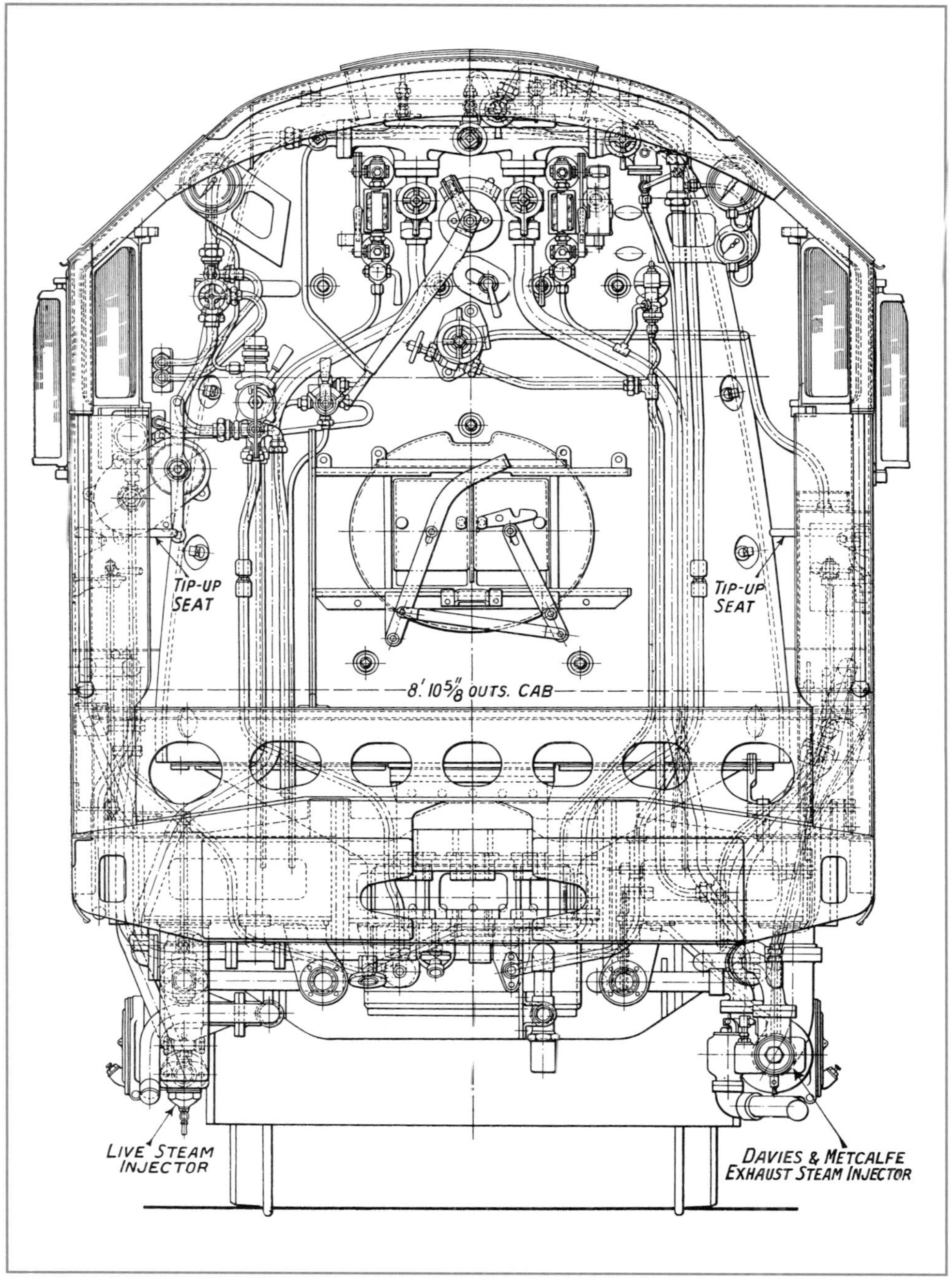

Figure 2: *General arrangement drawing of the cab.*
Railway Gazette

Plate 14 (above): *The rear of the tender. There are two main differences compared with the standard Stanier tender. Firstly the sides are extended towards the rear and end in a vertical line, to match the coaches and maintain the streamlined effect. Secondly, a coal pusher is fitted, indicated by the equipment on the back of the bunker; the horizontal box later had two short pipes fitted to vent exhaust steam.* Railway Gazette

Plate 13 (top left): *Interior view of the tender. The steam ram of the coal pusher at the top of the tender forced the two horizontal blocks downwards and forwards and so pushed coal towards the fireman. On the left, at the top under the coping is the bulge of the fire-iron tunnel.* Railway Gazette

Plate 15 (left): *The front of the tender. On the left in the picture is the hand brake; above it is the opening of the fire-iron tunnel, on the side of which is the steam control for the coal pusher. On the right is the handle operating the scoop. Above it is the engine-men's locker and to the right of that is the water gauge.* National Railway Museum

Plates 16 and 17: *Tender No. 9801 in Crewe Works yard after being brought out of the paint shop in May 1939.* W. Potter

Plate 18: *Broadside view of* Coronation *on completion and in photographic grey paint, as are the three photogaphs following.*

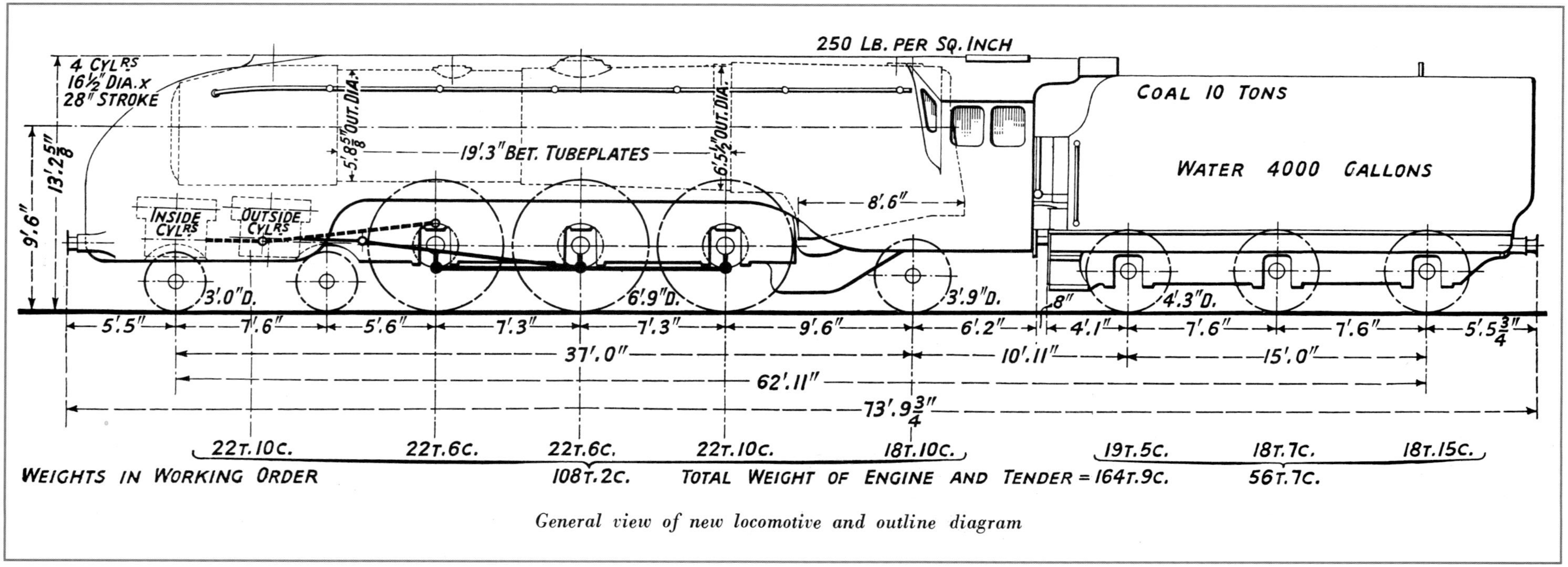

Figure 3: *Outline diagram of* Coronation.

Railway Gazette

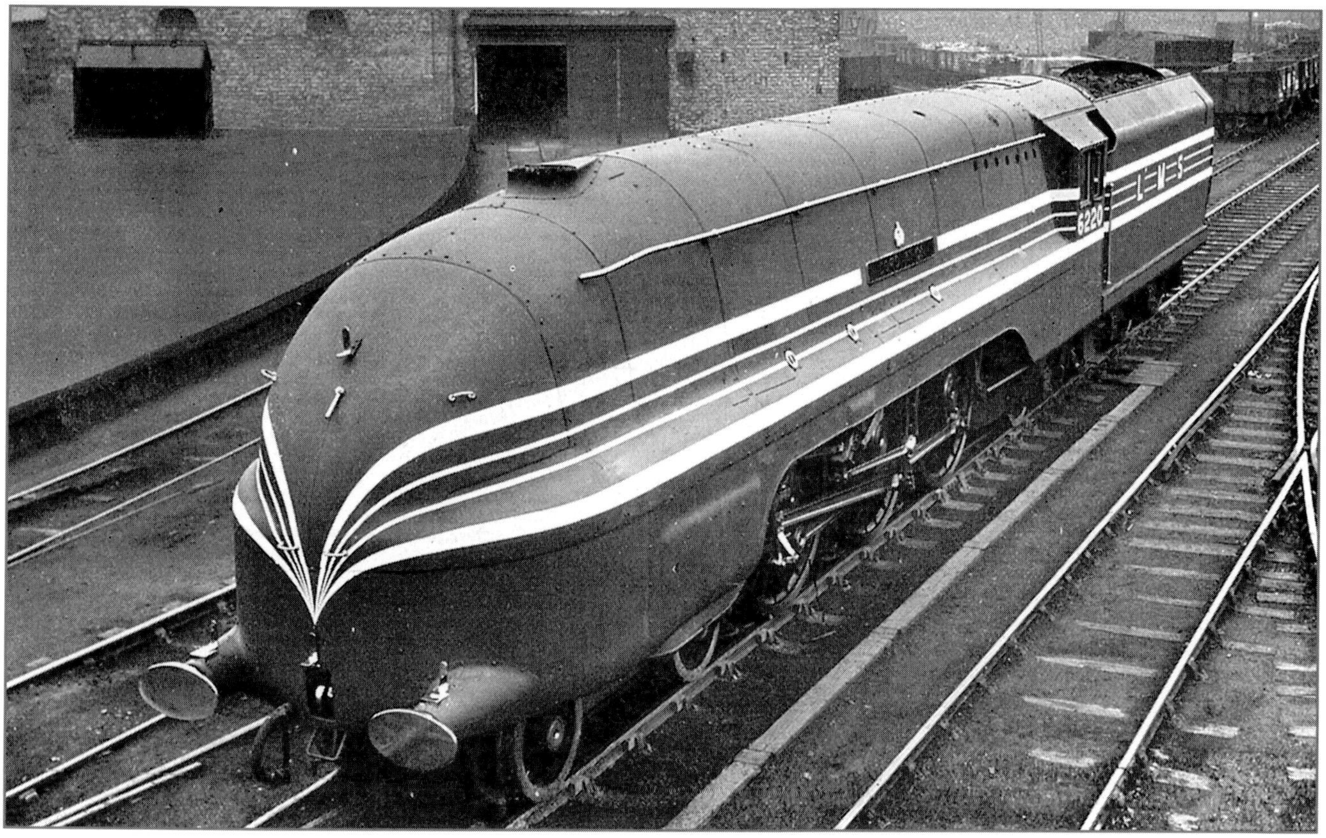

Plate 19: Coronation *posed with the Steel Foundry in the background and the Paint Shop behind the camera.* Railway Gazette

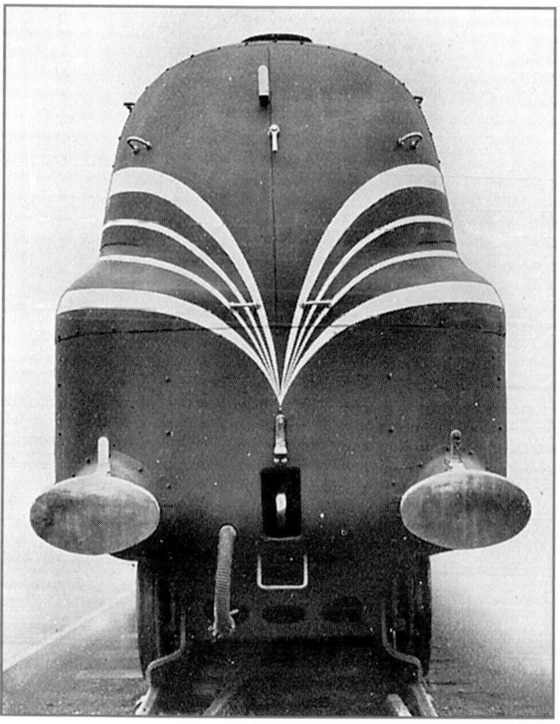

Plates 20 and 21: *Two views of* Coronation *showing the way the streamlined casing opened to give access to the smokebox door. Buffers are finished bright and lamp-irons and handles are nickel-plated. There is only one footstep beneath the front coupling, whereas photographs taken soon afterwards show two.* Railway Gazette

Plate 22: *General view of the new train. Nearest to the camera is brake first No. 5052. This picture and those which follow were taken on 21st May 1937.* Railway Gazette

moulding and ceiling presenting a very clean appearance which gives a sense of space. No projecting mouldings are employed but inlaid horizontal bands at cornice height and running through the seat ends are finished in dark contrasting timbers. Different timbers are used in each car, and the first-class vestibule dining cars are of different timbers in each train. The furnishings and trimmings are carried out in blue, green and brown, each train being made up of vehicles of one colour. The first-class trimming material gives a broche effect and the third-class an uncut moquette. Wilton carpets are used in the first-class corridor and vestibule cars and in the third-class vestibule cars, and heavy-quality brown cork lino in the third-class corridor cars. Curtains are fitted in the first-class and blinds in the third-class cars to harmonise with the colour scheme of each train.

Every compartment in the corridor first and corridor brake cars is finished differently, the timbers used being Australian maple butt, Queensland maple, South American prima-vera sunray, English olive ash (curly grain) and Australian walnut. The walls of the first-class vestibule dining cars are finished in light-coloured timbers and a very striking contrast effect has been obtained by using darker coloured veneers for the saloon doors. In the first train the first-class dining-car walls are covered with a very rich satin walnut and the large flush doors with claro-walnut, which is veneered to show a light circle in the centre of the door surrounded by the dark grained timber. The first-class vestibule car for the second train is finished in Canadian mountain maple with doors veneered in Nigerian kevazingo. The particularly fine waterfall grain of the kevazingo is shown off to good effect on the flush panelled doors.

In the first-class vestibule for the third train the contrast between the doors and walls is not so marked, the walls being veneered in straight-grained English olive ash and the doors in curly-grained English olive ash. The three third-class vestibule cars in each train are finished flush with horizontal inlaid bands similar to first-class cars but each car is finished in different timbers as follows: English weathered sycamore and English burry sycamore; English curly oak butt and English brown oak with tiger stripe; and Canadian silver elm. The veneer for the latter was cut from piles recovered from Waterloo Bridge, which had been under water from the time when the bridge was erected in 1817 until it was demolished in 1936. The third-class brakes are finished in South American peroba with contrasting inlaid horizontal bands of walnut. The metal fittings are finished in satin matt chrome in the first-class cars and oxidised Venetian bronze in the third-class cars, while throughout the trains the ceilings are covered in cream rexine.

The electric lighting is designed both to give the maximum efficiency and to harmonise with the general scheme of decoration. In the first-class vestibule cars a continuous tubular strip light is fitted in the ceilings of the saloons. This is supplemented with small tubular architectural lamps above the seats against the cross partitions, and a cylindrical stand lamp on every window sill. One 36in tubular strip light is fitted in the ceiling above every set of tables in the third-class vestibule dining cars and architectural lamps are provided above the seat backs on the cross partitions. Candle lamps with independent switches are fitted above every seat in the first-class corridor compartments, as well as an architectural lamp in the ceiling. Shoulder lights are fitted above the seat backs in the third-class corridor compartments with a separate light in the ceiling. Tubular architectural lamps are used throughout in the corridors and lavatories.

The lavatories throughout the train are finished flush; they have dark blue Rexine doors and walls up to the window-sills, silver Rexine above, and cream Rexine ceilings. The wash basins are pale blue porcelain with chromium plated taps and metal fittings, and the lavatory floors are laid with blue and white terazzo mosaic.

Contractors

The following firms supplied equipment for the coaches:

Decorative woods	Aeronautical Panel & Plywood Company; Laminated Wood Products Limited
Upholstery and carpets	T. F. Firth & Sons Ltd
Curtains	Courtaulds Limited
Rexine	ICI (Rexine) Ltd
Lamps	General Electric Co Ltd; London & Provincial Electrical Co Ltd
Blue and silver paint for train exterior	Docker Brothers
Pressure heating and ventilation	Thermotank Limited

Plate 23: *First-class vestibule diner No. 7507.* Railway Gazette

Plate 24: *Interior of first-class vestibule diner.* Railway Gazette

Plate 25: *Interior of third-class vestibule diner.* Railway Gazette

Plate 26: *First-class corridor coach No. 1069.* National Railway Museum

Plate 27 (left): *Interior of first-class corridor compartment.* Railway Gazette

Plate 28 (right): *Interior of third-class corridor compartment.* Railway Gazette

Plate 29: *Third-class corridor brake No. 5812.* National Railway Museum

Plate 30: *First-class corridor brake No. 5052.*
National Railway Museum

Plate 31: *Interior of compartment in first class corridor brake No. 5052.*
National Railway Museum

Plate 32: *Kitchen Car No. 30084.*
National Railway Museum

Plate 33: *Interior of compartment in third-class corridor brake No. 5812.* National Railway Museum

Plate 34: *Interior of third-class vestibule coach.* National Railway Museum

Plate 35: *Third-class vestibule coach No. 8996.* National Railway Museum

Four views of 'Coronation Scot' carriages taken on 31st May 1938. The most noticeable change is that separate carriage headboards are no longer carried. Instead the legend 'The Coronation Scot' is now painted directly on the carriage sides.

All - National Railway Museum

Plate 36: *First-class corridor brake No. 5053.*

Plate 37: *Third-class vestibule dining car No. 9004.*

Plate 38: *First-class vestibule dining car No. 7509.*

Plate 39: *Kitchen car No. 30089.*

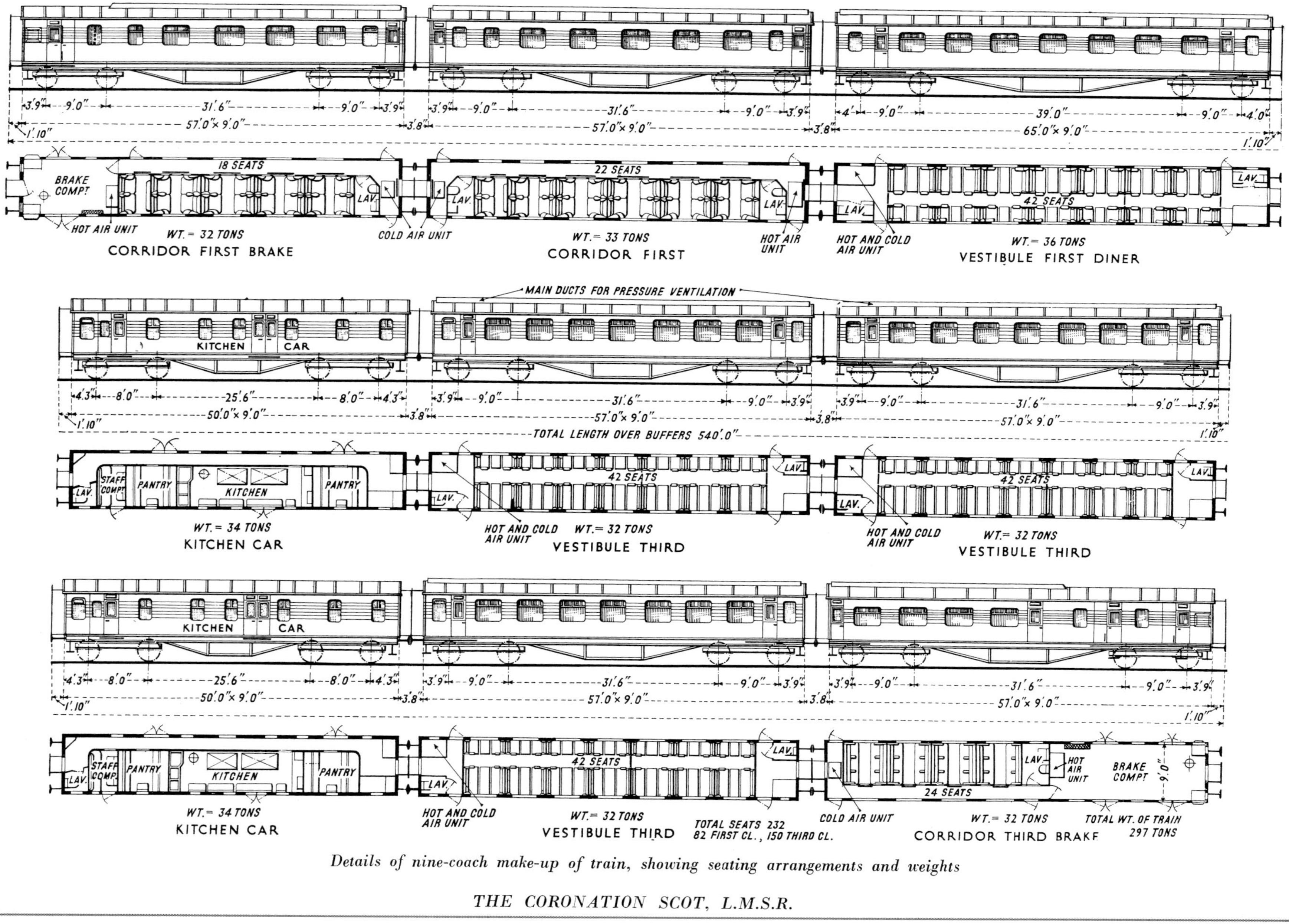

Figure 4: *Diagram of a nine-coach 'Coronation Scot' train, showing seating arrangements and weights.*

Railway Gazette

The Train Sets

The description in *The Railway Gazette* might give the impression that all the coaches were built new for 'The Coronation Scot' service. In fact, most of them had been built a short time previously. The LMS standard designs provided a good level of comfort and it was felt unnecessary to build new vehicles of every type. Selected coaches were therefore taken into Wolverton for modification, the fitting of air-conditioning (or rather of a pressure heating and ventilation system), new furnishings and such like, and to be repainted for use on the new service.

Enough coaches were provided to enable three nine-coach sets to be made up, two of which were in service at any one time and one spare. By modern standards it seems an extravagant waste of resources and extremely poor utilisation of stock to have two sets covering 400 miles per day each and one set doing nothing; but it has only been since the Beeching era that such importance has been placed on the maximum use of stock. Before then the emphasis was on the provision of adequate capacity to meet traffic needs and it was accepted that some stock would lie idle at times so as to be available for increases in traffic. 'Coronation Scot' sets were used at busy times for a Saturday Euston-Llandudno train, returning on Sunday, and for the Saturday down 'Mid-day Scot', W97. Quite probably the utilisation of 'The Coronation Scot' stock was no better and no worse than the average for the day.

Each set had a seating capacity of 82 first-class and 150 third-class passengers. Except for the kitchen cars and the open thirds, three vehicles of each type were provided so that there was one of each type for each set. Two kitchen cars were needed for each set, so six in all were provided; and there were nine open thirds, three for each set. The list below shows the vehicle types and numbers of the three sets.

Set	BFK	FK	RFO	RK	RTO	RTO	RK	RTO	BTK
1	5052	1069	7507	30084	8996	8993	30086	8961	5812
2	5053	1070	7508	30089	9003	9006	30085	9004	5792
3	5054	1071	7509	30087	8950	9029	30088	8931	5814

Plate 40: Coronation *backing the empty stock of the return Crewe-Euston record run out of Euston on 29th June 1937.*
LCGB Ken Nunn collection

Plate 41: *No. 6220* Coronation *passing Basford Hall Junction south of Crewe at the start of the climb to Whitmore with the up 'Coronation Scot' in the summer of 1937.* E. R. Morten

Chapter Two
HIGH SPEED AND REGULAR SERVICE

On completion *Coronation* was photographed by the official photographer and shown to the press at Crewe. It was run in on the usual turns to Shrewsbury and then with the new train put on display to the public at Euston during the latter part of June.

The World Speed Record

Then on 29th June came the famous test trip between Euston and Crewe. This trip occurred the day before the LNER ran a similar trip with its new high-speed train the 'Coronation'. Cecil J. Allen reported both trips in the August issue of *The Railway Magazine*. His introduction asserted that 'it would hardly be possible to crowd into two consecutive days more sensations in the realm of locomotive performance than the LMS and LNE authorities succeeded in doing on their trial runs of 29th and 30th June'. His account of the LMS trip was as follows:

'As the second kitchen car was not required on the trip, it had been cut out of the train, leaving eight vehicles of a tare weight of 263 tons, and the passenger complement brought the gross load to 270 tons behind the tender. The presence of that acknowledged Crewe expert, Driver T. J. Clark, at the regulator ensured that the best possible would be obtained from No. 6220 *Coronation*, and he was ably backed by Fireman J. Lewis.

'A fairly gentle start was made to Willesden, but the gradual acceleration to 82mph up the 1 in 339 to Carpender's Park, and the sustained $80\frac{1}{2}$ on the upper part of the 1 in 335 to Tring, gave good promise of what was to come. A general limit of 90mph had been imposed as far as Norton Bridge, however, and schedule times were not to be greatly departed from on the down journey, so that most of the downhill speeds were but little higher than those uphill, reminding one strongly of Paris-Orleans running in France. Another good uphill recovery was from Weedon, passed at a reduced speed of 77mph, up 1 in 490-350 to 82mph, then falling to 78 at the summit of the latter grade. It was a novel experience to travel from Polesworth to Tamworth at 75 to 77mph, after the years during which the pitfall check, now happily abolished, has operated here. Queensville curve at Stafford was taken, however, with speed right down to 30mph, and no attempt was made to get again into high speed until Norton Bridge had been cleared.

'From here the performance was electrifying indeed. Up the 1 in 509-650 from Norton Bridge to Standon Bridge speed rose from 60 to $75\frac{1}{2}$mph, and up the ensuing 1 in 590-398 ($2\frac{3}{4}$ miles of the latter) to Whitmore troughs to 85mph. A table and graph are given of the next 8 miles, between posts 148 and 156, from which it will be seen that the mile from post 155 to post 156 was covered in precisely 32 seconds, which gives an average speed of 112.5mph. The recorders all agreed as to the probability of a slight "peak" of 113mph and accepted this as the authentic maximum, exactly tieing with the 113mph of the LNER *Silver Fox*, and with both engines - a remarkable coincidence this - hauling an identical load of 270 tons (for the dynamome-

Plate 42: *No. 6220 awaiting departure from Crewe on a running in turn to Shrewsbury about the end of May 1937. The driver seems to be in discussion on some technical matter with a fitter from the works who is probably riding on the engine while running in. Because the casing behind the chimney tapered to a point, the chimney appears to be shaped differently when viewed from different angles.* Bournemouth Railway Club, W. H. G. Kelland collection

Plate 43: *After running in,* Coronation *was put on display at Euston for publicity purposes. It is seen here being backed into the station by a former LNWR 'Cauliflower' 0-6-0 on 24th June 1937. Sacking has been put over the buffers to preserve their pristine condition.*
LCGB Ken Nunn collection

ter car was added to "The Silver Jubilee" set on the test run of 27th August 1936) and on a very similar gradient. The Hasler recorder on the locomotive displayed a peak of 114mph, and it is a tribute to the accuracy of this appliance that it should have shown agreement within 1mph, at so tremendous a speed, with the figures obtained by three independent observers off the mileposts. Speed ranged at or above 100mph from post $151^{3}/_{4}$ to $156^{1}/_{4}$ ($4^{1}/_{2}$ miles), and averaged 100mph for 10 miles (147 to 157). Whether any higher speed could have been reached had a little more space been available for its development is problematical; from the trend of the acceleration curve it certainly seems possible. But at 113mph, we were within a couple of miles of Crewe, and the next problem on the footplate was that of stopping this thunderbolt in time. The engine was superbly handled here, and though we certainly took the first crossover at a higher than normal speed, the excellence of the track layout brought us into the platform with no worse casualties than a few unexpected embraces of passengers preparing to alight. Crewe was thus reached in 129min 46sec from Euston, $5^{1}/_{4}$min early, at an average start-to-stop speed of 73.1mph.

'The return journey was an extraordinary performance. "The shape of things to come" was seen in the acceleration up to Whitmore, whereby $71^{1}/_{2}$mph was attained up the 1 in 269 to Betley Road, 74 up the 3 miles at 1 in 177 to Madeley, and $80^{1}/_{2}$ up the final 1 in 348 to Whitmore troughs, Whitmore, 10.5 entirely uphill miles from Crewe, being thus cleared in the merest shade over "even time". From here onwards 90mph, or slightly over, was the ruling speed wherever possible, both downhill and on the level, and very little less uphill, as witness the drop only from 90 to 86 up $3^{1}/_{2}$ miles at 1 in 320 from Nuneaton to Bulkington. The acceleration from 40 to 75mph up the 1 in 370 from the Rugby slack to Kilsby tunnel was another fine effort. But it was after Stowe Hill tunnel, beyond Weedon, that the engine was really opened out, and this resulted in a maximum of exactly 100mph down the gentle declivity from Roade to Castlethorpe, partly 1 in 410 and partly 1 in 330. Here the 100mph was steadily maintained for $1^{1}/_{2}$ miles (posts $55^{1}/_{2}$ to 54), ending at Castlethorpe troughs. A time of 10min 13sec for the 15 miles from Bletchley up to Tring - including a slack to 85 through Leighton! - was again an astonishing feat, and we only fell short of another "100" by a mere mile an hour at King's Langley. Just after Willesden we overtook "The Lancastrian", suffering the indignity of slow road travel to keep out of our way, and, with every window from one end to the other a mass of spectators, looking for all the world like a travelling grandstand.

'So we rolled into Euston and stopped precisely 119min to the second after leaving Crewe, and 16min ahead of our scheduled arrival. Rugby had proved an exact half-way point in time, 59min 27sec from Crewe to Rugby, and 59min 33sec from Rugby to Euston. Only by 0.3sec had we escaped maintaining a start-to-stop average of 80mph from Crewe to Euston; 79.7mph was the precise figure, but over the 150.3 miles from Betley Road to Kilburn, including both Stafford and Rugby slacks, the average was as high 83.3mph. Best of all, however, was the average of 89.0mph over the 72.3 miles from Welton to Kilburn, although even yet this does not quite equal the previous British record of this kind - the 91.8mph of the LNER "Silver Jubilee" on its test run of 27th September 1935, sustained over the 70 miles from Wood Green to Fletton Junction, and over a line with considerable lengths of 1 in 200 gradient, as compared with the maximum steepness of 1 in 330 on the LMS. In favour of the LMS, however, was a trainload of 270 tons, as compared with the LNER 230 tons. It only remains to add an appreciation of the perfect smoothness of running even at 100mph and over, a witness to the value of the extensive programme of curve readjustment carried out by the LMS engineers, as well as to the excellence of the coach suspension. It is noteworthy that "The Coronation Scot" coaches have cylindrical wheel treads instead of the normal type coned to 1 in 20.'

In writing this account Cecil J. Allen was forced to choose his words carefully. He had been invited to travel on the train as an official observer, as one of three expert train-timers whose job was to make a record of the running, the other two being D. S. M. Barrie and S. P. W. Corbett. He therefore had no choice but to be diplomatic and so his description of the approach to Crewe skated delicately over what had actually happened.

The truth was that in his determination to capture the LNER record Driver Clark had delayed braking as long as possible. Thus his speed through the first crossover was 57mph instead of the prescribed 25mph, and it was largely thanks to the design of the locomotive's suspension, the quality of the track and good luck

Plate 44: *A familiar but striking view of the test run, taken from above the entrance to Watford tunnel - the driver is blowing the whistle to warn anyone inside the tunnel of the train's approach.* Courtesy Dr Adrian H. Collyns

LMS Trial Trip of 'Coronation Scot' Euston - Crewe
29th June 1937

Engine: 4-6-2 No. 6220 *Coronation*
Driver: T. J. Clark; Fireman: J. Lewis (Crewe)
Load: 8 cars, 263 tons tare, 270 tons gross

Distance miles		Schd min	Actual min	Actual sec	Speeds mph
0.0	EUSTON	0	0	00	-
1.0	Milepost 1	-	2	39	+32
3.0	Kilburn	-	5	29	54
5.4	WILLESDEN JC	8	7	53	68
8.1	Wembley	-	10	05	76
11.4	Harrow	-	12	27	79
13.3	HatchEnd	-	14	04	82
17.4	WATFORDJC	18	17	02	86½
20.9	King'sLangley	-	19	40	82
24.5	HemelHempstead	-	22	20	80½
28.0	Berkhamstead	-	24	55	80½
31.7	TRING	30	27	45	80½
36.1	Cheddington	-	30	55	87½
40.2	Leighton	-	33	56	*75
46.7	BLETCHLEY	41	38	57	82
52.4	Wolverton	-	43	08	6/*77½
54.8	Castlethorpe	-	44	57	79
59.9	Roade	51	48	56	76½
62.8	BLISWORTH	53fi	51	09	86
69.7	Weedon	-	56	20	*77
75.3	Welton	-	60	38	82/78
80.3	Hillmorton	-	64	23	85
82.6	RUGBY	70	66	28	*39
83.2	RugbyNo.7	-	67	35	*38
88.1	Brinklow	-	72	20	79
91.4	Shilton	-	74	47	82
93.5	Bulkington	-	76	27	79
97.1	NUNEATON	82	79	05	83
102.3	Atherstone	-	83	08	*72
106.5	Polesworth	-	86	33	75
110.0	TAMWORTH	94	89	24	77/*73
116.3	LICHFIELD	99	94	25	76½/72
121.0	Armitage	-	98	10	80 ½
124.3	Rugeley	106	100	46	*71
127.2	Colwich	-	103	20	*60
129.5	Milford	-	105	29	70½
133.1	StaffordNo.1	-	108	59	*30
133.6	STAFFORD	115	109	56	*30
136.9	GreatBridgeford	-	113	43	58½
138.9	NortonBridge	120	115	45	60
143.4	StandonBridge	-	119	44	75 ½
147.6	Whitmore	127	122	48	85
150.1	Madeley	-	124	27	94½
153.3	BetleyRoad	-	126	25	108
156.0	Milepost156	-	127	53	113
157.0	Milepost157	-	128	27	-
158.1	CREWE	135	129	46	-

*Service slack.
+At summit of Camden Bank.

LMS Trial Trip of 'Coronation Scot' Crewe - Euston
29thJune1937

Engine: 4-6-2 No. 6220 *Coronation*
Driver: T. J. Clark; Fireman: J. Lewis (Crewe)
Load: 8 cars, 263 tons tare, 270 tons gross

Distance miles		Schd min	Actual min	Actual sec	Speeds mph
0.0	CREWE	0	0	00	-
1.1	Milepost 157	-	2	23	-
4.8	Betley Road	-	6	06	71½
8.0	Madeley	-	8	44	74
10.5	Whitmore	11	10	42	+80½
14.7	Standon Bridge	-	13	32	90
19.2	NortonBridge	18	16	51	*74
21.2	Great Bridgeford	-	18	25	82
24.5	STAFFORD	23	20	58	-
25.0	Stafford No. 1	-	21	45	*30
28.6	Milford	-	25	13	75
30.9	Colwich	-	27	05	80/*71
33.8	Rugeley	31	29	18	90
37.1	Armitage	-	31	02	88
41.8	LICHFIELD	37	34	44	-
44.6	Hademore	-	36	36	92/89
48.1	TAMWORTH	42	38	55	90
51.6	Polesworth	-	41	27	*78
55.8	Atherstone	-	44	41	83/*71
61.0	NUNEATON	54	48	29	90
64.6	Bulkington	-	50	58	86
66.7	Shilton	-	52	29	93½
70.0	Brinklow	-	54	42	*85
74.9	Rugby No. 7	-	58	25	88½/*40
75.5	RUGBY	66	59	27	*40
77.8	Hillmorton	-	61	51	67½
79.9	Kilsby North End	-	63	35	75
82.8	Welton	-	65	46	86
88.4	Weedon	-	69	41	92/*79
95.3	BLISWORTH	82	74	24	92
98.2	Roade	84	76	22	88½
103.3	Castlethorpe	-	79	36	100
105.7	Wolverton	88½	81	08	*83
111.4	BLETCHLEY	93	85	10	89
117.9	Leighton	-	89	32	93/*85
122.0	Cheddington	-	92	21	89/87
126.4	TRING	107	95	23	86½
130.1	Berkhamstead	-	97	59	90/*85
133.6	HemelHempstead	-	100	16	93
137.2	King's Langley	-	102	30	99
140.7	WATFORD JC	117½	104	53	*84
144.8	Hatch End	-	107	45	85
146.7	Harrow	-	109	00	96
150.0	Wembley	-	11	105	95
152.7	WILLESDEN JC	127	112	50	*85
155.1	Kilburn	-	114	33	*79
157.1	Milepost 1	-	116	57	-
158.1	EUSTON	135	119	00	-

+On Whitmore troughs, at summit of Madeley bank.
*Service slack.

LMS Trial Trip of 'CoronationScot'
The Record Length

Mileposts ex Euston	Passing Times min	Passing Times sec	Differences sec	Speeds mph
148	123	16.8	-	-
148½	123	37.6	20.8	86.5
149	123	58.0	20.4	88.2
149½	124	7.8	19.8	90.9
150	124	27.0	19.2	93.6
150½	124	46.0	19.0	94.5
151	125	4.6	18.6	96.8
151½	125	22.8	18.2	98.9
152	125	40.4	17.6	102.3

Mileposts ex Euston	Passing Times min	Passing Times sec	Differences sec	Speeds mph
152½	125	57.8	17.4	103.4
153	126	14.8	17.0	105.9
153½	126	31.4	16.8	107.1
154	126	48.0	16.6	108.4
154½	127	4.4	16.4	109.8
155	127	20.6	16.2	111.1
155½	127	36.6	16.0	112.5
156	127	52.6	16.0	112.5
157	128	27.0	Steam off	

that no derailment occurred. As it was, the passengers were thrown about somewhat more violently than the phrase 'unexpected embraces' implies and there were breakages in the dining car. It might be argued that Driver Clark had clearly judged his braking perfectly but things might easily have been otherwise. A spectacularly disastrous end to the attempt on the speed record may well have had an adverse effect on the high-speed programme on the LMS and perhaps also on the LNER.

In the event, everything proceeded according to plan. The LMS claimed the world speed record for steam on the strength of Driver Clark's effort. It based its claim on the maximum reading of 114mph given by the Hasler recorder, which beat the record of *Silver Fox* by just 1mph. The three official recorders agreed on a maximum speed of 113mph. Whether or not the company's claim was reasonable is debatable. Learned articles have appeared in the railway press from time to time by such authorities as Professor W. A. Tuplin asserting that the stopwatch method of train-timing, of which Cecil J. Allen was undoubtedly an expert, was incapable of giving the accuracy that was claimed for it. Similarly, no doubt, the accuracy of the recorder could be questioned. Whatever the truth of the matter, however, the LNER followed the LMS example the following year. When *Mallard* broke the LMS record, the speed of 126mph given by the recorder was claimed as the new world speed record rather than the 125mph calculated by the stopwatch timers.

No further attempts on the record were made by the LMS and it remains unknown whether a 'Coronation' Pacific was capable of breaking the LNER record. The later double-chimney engines represented a considerable advance on the single-chimney design of *Coronation* in much the same way as *Mallard* with its Kylchap double chimney was an advance on the single-chimney *Silver Fox*. Unfortunately, it will never now be known exactly how large that advance was in terms of miles per hour.

Plate 45: *No. 6220* Coronation *passing Carpenders Park on the high-speed test run of 29th June 1937. The train left Euston at 9.50am. Above it is an accompanying aircraft carrying photographers.*
LCGB Ken Nunn collection

Plate 46: *The test train north of Rugeley Trent Valley. Just over thirty two miles later an official speed of 114mph was reached on the descent to Crewe.* P. S. Kendrick

Plate 47: *Successful return to Euston. Driver Clark is congratulated by an LMS official, thought to be Vice President F. A. Lemon, while William Stanier himself and Fireman John Lewis, both smiling broadly, look on.*

THE CORONATION SCOT

POINT-TO-POINT MILEAGES, RUNNING TIMES AND SPEEDS

EUSTON - CARLISLE - GLASGOW

Distance from EUSTON Miles	STATION	p.m.	Point-to-Point Time Mins.	Point-to-Point Distance Miles	Point-to-Point Speed M.P.H.
0.0	Euston ... ... dep.	1 30			
5.4	Willesden ... pass	1 39	9	5.4	36.0
17.5	Watford ... ... pass	1 50	11	12.1	66.0
31.7	Tring ... ... pass	2 3	13	14.2	65.5
46.7	Bletchley ... ... pass	2 15	12	15.0	75.0
59.9	Roade ... ... pass	2 26	11	13.2	72.0
82.5	Rugby ... ... pass	2 46	20	22.7	68.1
97.1	Nuneaton ... ... pass	3 0	14	14.6	62.6
116.3	Lichfield ... ... pass	3 17	17	19.2	67.8
124.3	Rugeley ... ... pass	3 23	6	8.0	80.0
133.6	Stafford ... ... pass	3 32	9	9.3	62.0
158.1	Crewe ... ... pass	3 54	22	24.5	66.8
182.1	Warrington ... pass	4 16	22	24.0	65.5
193.9	Wigan ... ... pass	4 28	12	11.8	59.0
209.0	Preston ... ... pass	4 44	16	15.1	56.6
230.0	Lancaster ... ... pass	5 4	20	21.0	63.0
236.3	Carnforth ... pass	5 9	5	6.3	75.6
249.1	Oxenholme ... pass	5 21	12	12.8	64.0
262.2	Tebay ... ... pass	5 36	15	13.1	52.4
267.7	Shap Summit ... pass	5 44	8	5.5	41.3
281.2	Penrith ... ... pass	5 56	12	13.5	67.5
299.1	Carlisle ... arr. / dep.	6 13 / 6 15	17	17.9	63.2
307.7	Gretna ... ... pass	6 24	9	8.6	56.2
338.8	Beattock ... ... pass	6 49	25	31.1	74.6
348.8	Beattock Summit pass	7 4	15	10.0	40.0
366.0	Symington ... pass	7 19	15	17.2	68.8
372.6	Carstairs ... ... pass	7 25	6	6.6	66.0
388.5	Motherwell ... pass	7 42	17	15.9	56.1
401.4	**Glasgow** ... ... arr.	8 0	**18**	**12.9**	**43.0**

OVER-ALL AVERAGE SPEED 61.7 M.P.H.

THE CORONATION SCOT

POINT-TO-POINT MILEAGES, RUNNING TIMES AND SPEEDS

GLASGOW - CARLISLE - EUSTON

Distance from GLASGOW Miles	STATION	p.m.	Point-to-Point Time Mins.	Point-to-Point Distance Miles	Point-to-Point Speed M.P.H.
0.0	Glasgow ... ... dep.	1 30			
12.9	Motherwell ... pass	1 49	19	12.9	40.8
28.8	Carstairs ... ... pass	2 10	21	15.9	45.4
35.4	Symington ... pass	2 16	6	6.6	66.0
52.6	Beattock Summit pass	2 32	16	17.2	64.5
62.6	Beattock ... ... pass	2 42	10	10.0	60.0
93.7	Gretna ... ... pass	3 7	25	31.1	74.6
102.3	Carlisle ... arr. / dep.	3 15 / 3 17	8	8.6	64.5
120.2	Penrith ... ... pass	3 38	21	17.9	51.1
133.7	Shap Summit ... pass	3 53	15	13.5	54.0
139.2	Tebay ... ... pass	3 58	5	5.5	66.0
152.3	Oxenholme ... pass	4 10	22	13.1	65.5
165.1	Carnforth ... pass	4 21	11	12.8	69.8
171.4	Lancaster ... ... pass	4 26	5	6.3	75.6
192.4	Preston ... ... pass	4 45	19	21.0	66.7
207.5	Wigan ... ... pass	5 2	17	15.1	53.3
219.3	Warrington ... pass	5 14	12	11.8	59.0
243.3	Crewe ... ... pass	5 36	22	24.0	65.5
267.8	Stafford ... ... pass	6 0	24	24.5	61.3
277.1	Rugeley ... ... pass	6 9	9	9.3	62.0
285.1	Lichfield ... ... pass	6 15	6	8.0	80.0
304.3	Nuneaton ... pass	6 32	17	19.2	67.8
318.9	Rugby ... ... pass	6 46	14	14.6	62.6
341.5	Roade ... ... pass	7 6	20	22.7	68.1
354.7	Bletchley ... ... pass	7 17	11	13.2	72.0
369.7	Tring ... ... pass	7 31	14	15.0	64.3
383.9	Watford ... ... pass	7 42	11	14.2	77.5
396.0	Willesden ... pass	7 52	10	12.0	72.6
401.4	**Euston...** ... arr.	8 0	**8**	**5.4**	**40.5**

OVER-ALL AVERAGE SPEED 61.7 M.P.H.

Figure 5: *Timings of 'The Coronation Scot' reproduced from the official booklet* The Track of the Coronation Scot.

Plate 48: Coronation *leaving Euston on the inaugural run of 'The Coronation Scot' on 5th July 1937.*

Plate 49: *No. 6223* Princess Alice *leaving Euston with the down 'Coronation Scot' on 16th June 1938.*
F. W. Shuttleworth collection

Normal Service

So it was that 'The Coronation Scot' entered normal service, the inaugural runs taking place on 5th July. In contrast to the drama of the test run, the service immediately operated reliably and without sensation, and continued to do so until the outbreak of the Second World War. While the railway journals often reported some exciting occurrence on the LNER high-speed workings, they featured the working of 'The Coronation Scot' much less frequently.

The main reason for this was, of course, that in general the LNER trains were faster and so required harder work from the engines. For example, the LNER 'Coronation' was allowed six hours in either direction to cover the 392.8 miles between London and Edinburgh. Although 'The Coronation Scot' had to climb both Shap and Beattock, it still had a relatively easier schedule, $6^1/_2$ hours for the 401.4 miles between London and Glasgow. Because in general the LNER engines had to be driven harder, they were likely to provide far more interest to enthusiasts than a train which ran uneventfully to schedule day in and day out even though that train served its passengers just as well. Another factor, of course, was that the LNER operated more high-speed trains than the LMS anyway, and so the chances of newsworthy events occurring with them were that much greater.

Basically 'The Coronation Scot' was provided to serve passengers travelling between London and Carlisle and between London and Glasgow. Northbound it called at Carlisle to set down passengers only and southbound to pick up, so that passengers travelling between Carlisle and Glasgow were not carried. Seats could be reserved at Euston, Carlisle and Glasgow at a charge of 2s 6d for each journey. Engine crews were changed at Carlisle; Camden and Upperby men worked south of there and Polmadie men north.

The effect of the new service on the public was immediate and considerable. Crowds gathered at the lineside to see the train pass, and the adoption of streamlining and the special paint scheme were more than justified in publicity alone. The train captured the mood of the time in symbolising the end of recession and the approach of a new era of progress and prosperity. It also boosted the morale of the LMS work force since it showed that the company was able to compete successfully with anything done by its rivals.

It is more difficult nowadays to assess the impact which the train had on the travelling public it was designed to serve rather than on the public in general or the enthusiast. Fortunately in January 1938 the *Journal of the Stephenson Locomotive Society* contained some notes by S. H. Beaver, in which he gave his impressions of travelling on the train. Although an enthusiast, he records the things he particularly noticed as a passenger and which distinguished the train from the ordinary express train of the day.

He found that the most striking thing was the consistent high speed maintained uphill and down over the whole journey except for the ascents of Shap and Beattock. Most of the other adverse gradients seemed to produce little effect on the speed, nor did down gradients yield very high maximum speeds. The running itself was very smooth and the high speed was only really appreciated 'by timing or looking occasionally at one's watch' and observing the 'astonishing' distance

Plate 50: *Classic view of the down 'Coronation Scot' climbing Camden bank behind No. 6221* Queen Elizabeth *on 23rd September 1938. Separate carriage headboards have been replaced by the legend 'The Coronation Scot' painted directly on the carriages themselves. On the left is 'Jubilee' No. 5563* Australia *which has arrived on an up express. The stock is being taken to the carriage sidings by another engine and the 'Jubilee' is still coupled to what is now the rear of the train.* E. R. Wethersett

Plate 51: *The down 'Coronation Scot' near Euxton in April 1939, hauled by No. 6222* Queen Mary. E. R. Morten

Plate 52: *The up 'Coronation Scot' at Euxton in April 1939 hauled by No. 6229* Duchess of Hamilton *in blue livery; originally No. 6220* Coronation *it had exchanged identities at this time with the engine which went to America.* E. R. Morten

that had been covered in a given time. Because of the speed, some slacks occurred 'the existence of which one had never dreamt of before' such as the curves at Atherstone and at Norton Bridge; and the severe slacks at Rugby and Stafford appeared grossly exaggerated after travelling consistently at over 80mph for some time. The amount of permanent way ballast that was kicked or swept up at the end of troughs (perhaps through not picking up the scoop in time) and at places where the surface ballast had been disturbed by platelayers was rather frightening at times, creating a 'great rattle underneath the train and sometimes along the sides too'.

As regards passenger comfort, it was 'alternately too hot and too cold'. It was too hot because the attendants were never asked to 'control the temperature' and it was too cold because the 'English traveller was not yet educated up to air-conditioning' and persisted in throwing open a window as soon as he felt a little warm, causing intense inconvenience to passengers sitting behind him. As for eating, it was 'almost as bad as on board ship: as soon as lunch is finished, tea begins, and almost on top of tea comes dinner - not too good if one is cramped up in a seat for over six hours!'

An entirely different kind of account of a journey on 'The Coronation Scot' appeared in the London Midland and Scottish Railway Centenary Number of *The Times*, published on 20th September 1938. This was a splendidly lavish production of 28 pages, and in those days *The Times* used a page size which was considerably larger than it uses today, 18½in by 24½in. The whole of the front page was devoted to a striking head-on photograph of 'The Coronation Scot' at speed, while inside were comprehensive and authoritative articles on the company's history, technical developments, operations and areas of the country it served. Equally fascinating are the advertisements, some by the company promoting its services, such as its hotels, and others by manufacturers of railway equipment and by resorts seeking to attract travellers.

Among the articles was one entitled 'Two Famous Trains, Impressions of the Coronation Scot and Her Sister' by Naomi Royde-Smith. This is a description of a journey north from Euston to Glasgow by 'The Coronation Scot' and of the return journey south from Edinburgh to Euston by 'The Royal Scot' (the 'Sister' referred to in the title).

The article is of interest not so much for the technical information it contains, which is very little, but for the impressions the journey made on its author, the feeling she obviously had and tries to convey that this was the ultimate experience in rail passenger travel, comfort and speed. Also of interest, incidentally, is her style. By present-day standards it is pretentious and long-winded, and even perhaps in places self-consciously clever. That *The Times* regarded this as good style and appropriate for its readership is in itself significant, and indeed the style of the article is not exceptional but typical of that used throughout the special issue. At the same time, to the modern mind accustomed to 'investigative journalism' and 'balanced reporting', which is obliged to find something negative to comment on and indeed takes pleasure in doing so, it seems naively enthusiastic and approving; but perhaps it is none the worse for that.

The part of the article dealing with 'The Coronation Scot' is as follows:

'Sentimentality, snobbishness, romanticism, call the weakness by what name you please, will always make the passenger prefer to travel by a train with a name rather than by the 9.15, though few of us, except boys small enough to travel on half a ticket, bother our heads much about the engine which draws us. The 'Irish Mail', that most thrilling of all named trains, may run behind 'Kings' and 'Princes' and 'Great Regiments' for all the passenger cares: the passenger, in the main being querulously indifferent to any virtue but punctuality and the kind of sauce served with the fried fillet of plaice on the expresses in which he travels from one country to another.

'But even the most world-weary traveller must gaze with a brightening eye on that last word in named trains 'The Coronation Scot'. This blue and silver miracle consists of three nine-coach trains. One, upholstered in blue, leaves Euston every weekday except Saturday at 1.30; the other, its trimmings all green, leaves Glasgow at the same hour, to flash past one another at Preston and to reach Glasgow and Euston simultaneously at 8pm. The third co-equal member of this trinity, but distinguished from its fellows by the brownness of its interior colour scheme, relieves the strain of five journeys a week by doing two or three of them itself, in both directions. One of the trains is the one veneered with wood cut from the piles of old Waterloo Bridge, sea-

Plate 53: *No. 6224* Princess Alexandra *passing Preston with the down 'Coronation Scot' on 29th July 1937.* E. R. Morten

Plate 54: *No. 6224* Princess Alexandra *taking water from Dillicar Troughs just south of Tebay with the up 'Coronation Scot' on 30th August 1938.* Courtesy Adrian H. Collyns

Plate 55: *No. 6224* Princess Alexandra *passing Penrith Junction with the up train on 23rd August 1938.*
LCGB Ken Nunn collection

soned by a hundred and twenty years' immersion in the mud of the Thames, as a tablet makes known to the traveller. As the accommodation on these super-trains is limited to eighty-two first and one hundred and fifty third-class passengers, and as, at the height of the season, they are filled to capacity on each journey and seats in them must be booked days in advance, it is better not to let the captious passenger have the slightest excuse for assuming that any one train exceeds another in glory.

Blue and Silver

'I myself, having a mania for travelling by named trains, had hoped that my first journey on 'The Coronation Scot' would be in that combination of its eighteen coaches and five engines that was 'Coronation' throughout. Finding myself at Euston with 20 minutes to burn after my seat had been located and my suitcases disposed on end above it, I made my way from end to end of the austere and beautiful interior; passing through its well-found kitchens, discovering that the day's journey was to be made in the blue section, and that the third-class coaches were, by reason of their very slightly less decorated compartments, almost more inviting to travel in during hot weather than the first; also that the luggage van was relatively small because the 'Coronation' does not carry merchandise and its passengers are chiefly of the class that travels light; but when I came to the end of the foremost coach the engine was not there. She had been detained at her toilet in some shed beyond my ken, and it was not until I reached Glasgow and walked down the train once more, on the platform this time, that I saw the blue and silver monster, looking like some armoured leviathan with a dolphin's head; smooth; streamlined; without funnel or visible shaft above her rounded smokebox, the heroine who had climbed the steep ascent to Shap at 50 miles an hour and had reached a thousand feet above sea level at Beattock Summit at 41. She was not *Coronation*, but her sister and facsimile, No. 6224 *Princess Alexandra*. By this time I had seen too much, enjoyed too many travelling mercies, to feel any emotion but wonder and a slight curiosity about the very small cab-window, a tiny gill in the cetacean flank which appeared to be all the protection offered to the driver's countenance when he needed to attend to outside phenomena.

He's awa'

'He's awa',' said the being whom I mistook for the driver, and was awa' himself before I had time to ask him about this and other details of the journey. I was one of the crowd from whose curiosity this man had done well to escape. Even though he had only brought the 'Coronation' on from Carlisle, where the Euston driver had left her, he had brought her, and us, over a hundred see-saw miles in an hour and 40 minutes, and was entitled to call it a day.

'The main line from London to Scotland passes shuttlewise through the history of Great Britain. It runs for miles alongside the Grand Junction Canal; past Berkhampstead, with its rectory, the birthplace of William Cowper; past Abbot's Langley, where Nicholas Breakspear, the only Englishman who ever became Pope of Rome, was born, and past an anonymous highwayman's grave, before it is 30 miles from London. After Tring, visited by pious Americans because the births and deaths of various Washingtons are noted in the register of the parish church, it crosses the Icknield Way, and the traveller, who by this time has reached the second course of luncheon, will be paying less attention to the panorama outside than to his food. Also, after half an hour's progress from 35 miles an hour, as it leaves Willesden, 'The Coronation Scot' has settled down to the business of getting up speed. In the 15 miles between Tring and Bletchley, *Coronation* or *Princess Alexandra* or *Queen Elizabeth*, or one of their sisters *Queen Mary* and *Princess Alice*, begins to show her paces. In 12 minutes she has accelerated from 65 to 75 miles an hour, and at 75 miles an hour the countryside of Buckinghamshire looks less like scenery than a horizontally striped green wallpaper with a misty pattern of beech trees and churches spread on its agreeable surface.

'An hour later, possibly in order to give the passengers a chance of seeing the 'Ladies of the Vale', those three soft, rosy spires of Lichfield Cathedral which presided over the severities of Dr Johnson's boyhood, probably because the line curves a good deal at this point, the blue and silver train slows to a mere 62. She makes up for it five minutes later by dashing through Rugeley at her top notch of 80. This is not because she wishes to spare nervous passengers the shudder of remembering that, at Rugeley, William Palmer arranged to poison all about him in the middle years of the nineteenth century; but because the train has now entered the Vale of Trent. Ever since the beginning of railway time engine drivers have boasted to one another of the fewness of the minutes it has taken them 'to cross the Trent'. Today this quaint old custom is suspended. The 'Coronation Scot' does it in nine.

Through the Midlands

'The Midlands reveal their famous houses of which Pooley Hall, the inadequately named stronghold of Marmion, that super-hero of poetic romance, is less hidden from view by woodland and hillside than other large and equally historic mansions, and soon the cottage near Shallowford Village where Izaak Walton lived, and Meece Brook, in which he angled, may be seen; but only by those who have energy and courage enough to dash from one side of the coach to the other, which not only makes the dasher unpopular with fellow-passengers but is an effort undertaken not without risk of accident when the transit has to be made at right-angles to the headlong flight of the express.

'Indeed, by the time the northbound 'Coronation' has slowed down to 56 at Preston in order to hail her sister making south at 66.7, the passenger has probably given up the attempt to see anything at all for a time. I myself closed my eyes, once the southbound train had vanished and waited for the heavy panting of the engine and the slowing down of speed to warn me that we were in Cumberland and in sight of Helvellyn and Blencathra and Crossfell and of streams and pools and glens through which their waters fall down to the lakes beyond the mountains. But the engine made no sound more audible than the faint hum that had long grown inaudible under the quiet monotone of the wheels that carried us. When I opened them again we were at Grayrigg, where the Society of Friends built its first Meeting House. In a few minutes we should pass over the lovely gorge of the Upper Lune and be among traces of the Stone Age and the limestone crags of the Fells.

An Impious Feat

'We slowed down from 52 to 41 and reached the flat stretch at Shap summit. As we passed the monument erected at the time of another Coronation - a hundred and one years ago - I remembered that Queen Victoria, told that the train she had just left had at one moment of its journey attained the speed of 60 miles an hour, first refused to believe this statement, and then dictated a letter to those who were responsible for this quite impious feat, adjuring them to 'see that it did not happen again'.

'We may smile at this instance of royal obstructiveness, but I was not the only passenger in 'The Coronation Scot' who was glad of the two minutes' respite at Carlisle, where the driver who had brought us from Euston gave place to the one I failed to congratulate at Glasgow.

The very well documented guide and companion to the 'Coronation' and its wayside scenes states that, in the eight miles between Carlisle, where it stops, and Gretna, where it crosses the Border, this remarkable train works up its speed from 0 to 55.2. I was sure this was true, but, like Queen Victoria, I found it hard to believe. Then I remembered that, soon after we had crossed Shap summit, the shadow of what I took to be a rather wide bridge had fallen across the page on which I was making notes, and on referring to the guide discovered that it really was a tunnel. There are, it appears, ten tunnels on the line from London to Glasgow; one of these, between Welton and Rugby, is almost a mile and a half long; but when you travel at 75 miles an hour you have barely time to realise that you are in a tunnel before you are out of it, and this remains the only one I recognised for what it was throughout the journey, once we had got clear of Primrose Hill.

'The apparent absence of tunnels, the interesting change from the guard in dark blue and braid of other trains to the conductor in blue and silver on this one; the spaciousness and charm of the blue and silver lavatories paved with terrazzo mosaic; the large blue wash-basins; the lavish flow of hot and cold water from the chromium plated taps, are all things to remember with satisfaction. But quite the most entrancing luxury of all is provided, not for the passengers, but for the engine which, as I saw, scooped up from the troughs between the rails water specially softened for her digestion by huge cisterns on the banks.

In two points only does 'The Coronation Scot' overstep the bounds of travelling comfort. At 80 miles an hour it is impossible to resist the window-closing fellow-passenger and - even at 90 - which I suspect is

Plate 56: *The up 'Coronation Scot' leaving Glasgow Central behind No. 6220* Coronation. Photomatic

touched by the 'Queens' and 'Princesses' more often than the guide admits, her progress is so quiet and so steady that, unless you are very rude indeed, you cannot foil the conversational advances of that other human nuisance, the Chatty Stranger. To be honest, however, I must admit that my fellow-passenger up to Glasgow was so tactful in restraint and so amusing when the ice was broken that I was glad she spoke to me.'

As this article hints, from the outset the company made a considerable effort to publicise the service. In the public timetable the whole of the first page was devoted to it and moreover was distinctively printed with a Coronation blue background and special lettering. A special booklet was produced, *The Track of the Coronation Scot,* which contained 'a running commentary on the Journey from London to Glasgow by the West Coast Route'. It was written by Edmund Vale and was No. 3 in the 'LMS Book of the Train' series; No. 1 was *The Triumph of the Royal Scot* and No. 2 *The Story of the Irish Mail.* It contained a description of the engines and train, details of the mileages and timings and a description of the route showing all stations and all overbridges except footbridges 'to aid in identifying views and places' and information of things of interest to be seen and notes on 'the building of the line and of features of interest passed on the journey.'

The company also produced special 'Coronation Scot' books of matches. They were wider than the normal size today and so were a suitably horizontal format to accommodate a colour picture of the train on the front. On the back was the legend 'The Coronation Scot' in the same style of lettering as in the timetable and beneath it were the timings, '6½ hours' printed large for emphasis, and the name of the company. Along each match was printed one word in such a way that collectively the matches in the book conveyed the theme of the service: 'CORONATION', 'SCOT', 'STREAMLINED', 'COMFORT' and 'SPEED'.

Plate 57: *No. 6221* Queen Elizabeth *at Crewe North shed on 10th October 1937. With such long engines it was difficult for photographers to get an unobstructed broadside view.* W. H. Whitworth

Plate 58: *Another view on the same occasion, showing the streamlined lamps to advantage.* W. Leslie Good

A Problem on the Footplate

On 1st July 1937, before in fact the report on the design of the streamlining itself had been published, another report was issued by the Research Department, Engineering Section, Derby, dealing with an urgent problem that had arisen with the first of the new streamlined engines in service. Basically, the problem was that as the coal in the tender was used up, air travelling along the top of the engine was drawn downwards and forwards over the coal space, through the shovelling hole in the front of the tender and into the cab. The report is entitled 'Return Air Flow in "Coronation Princess Royal" Tender' and its introduction outlines the problem in the following words: 'Following reports from the CME Department that the occupants of the cab of the "Coronation Princess Royal" were suffering considerable discomfort from a continuous barrage of small coal particles, arising from the nature of the airflow over the tender coal space, wind tunnel tests were conducted to find means of alleviating the problem.'

In a normal engine air flowing along the sides of the boiler and cab enters the cab through the ventilator in the cab roof, the cab windows and the spaces above and below the doors. Most of it finds an exit through the shovelling hole in the front of the tender but some is drawn into the firebox through the firehole door. Tests were carried out in the wind tunnel with the usual 1/24 scale model and four variations were tried: with the standard hood between the cab roof and the front bulkhead of the tender removed; with the standard hood between the cab roof and the front bulkhead of the tender in its normal position; with the hood extended to cover the equivalent of 3ft of the coal space; and with the hood extended to cover the equivalent of 6ft of the coal space. In the first two cases air was drawn into the cab through the shovelling hole; in the other two cases it was drawn out of the cab through the shovelling hole.

The tests showed that in the streamlined engines when air was drawn into the cab it was because the normal flow was resisted by disturbed air behind the front bulkhead of the tender and was thereby in effect reversed. By fitting partial covers over the coal space, the source of this resistance could be moved further to the rear and so the normal outward flow of air through the shovelling hole could be established. It was suggested that a 6ft extension to the cab hood would solve the problem on the real engines and that this solution could be tested easily by using a wagon sheet as a makeshift tender cover. The report also pointed out that if a complete cover over the tender were to be adopted, it would not only solve the problem but would also produce a further reduction in the overall air resistance of the locomotive.

A partial cover extending about two feet over the tender was tried on engine No. 6224 *Princess Alexandra* and was found to be a failure. The results of the tests were contained in a report by the Research Department dated 22nd September 1937. Its conclusions were that draughts into the cab through the shovelling hole could be prevented only by a complete tender cover and not by a partial one. It was found, however, that if an upward projecting lip were fitted to a partial cover, the desired effect could be achieved and the air would flow from the cab to the tender. Various shapes and sizes of lips were tried and the conclusion was reached that 'the simplest type, consisting of a vertical flange or lip, gives as good results as any'. The ideal height for the lip was difficult to determine for various reasons such as fluc-

Plate 59: *No. 6221* Queen Elizabeth *passing Headstone Lane with the Royal Train on route from Holytown to Euston on 5th May 1938.* LCGB Ken Nunn collection

Plate 60: *No. 6222* Queen Mary *in the centre road at Shrewsbury. It has worked in from Crewe and is awaiting its return working.* A. G. Ellis collection

Plate 61: *No. 6224* Princess Alexandra *at Shrewsbury, taking water before returning to Crewe with a northbound train. This view shows well the difficulty facing the fireman when manhandling the bag of the water column through the opening in the side of the tender and into the tank filler. It would be particularly difficult when the bag was frozen stiff in winter.* A. G. Ellis collection

Plate 62: *The second batch of five streamlined Pacifics was painted in standard LMS crimson lake with gold bands. Here No. 6225* Duchess of Gloucester *in Crewe Works in 1938.*
L. Hobdey, courtesy Michael Bentley

Plate 63: *A close-up view of the front end of* Duchess of Gloucester *on the same occasion.*
Leonard Hobdey, courtesy Michael Bentley

Plate 64: *Rear view of* Duchess of Gloucester *on Crewe North shed, 7th May 1939.* A. G. Ellis collection

Plate 65: *No. 6223* Princess Alice *at Shrewsbury on the usual fill-in turn. To paint the lining on these engines Crewe Works re-employed a number of skilled painters who had been sacked during the depression of the late 1920s and early 1930s.*
A. G. Ellis collection

Plate 66: *Nameplate of No. 6225, on 14th August 1938.* L. Hanson

Plate 67: *No. 6225* Duchess of Gloucester, *awaits the arrival of a northbound train at Shrewsbury before working it to Crewe.*
A. G. Ellis collection

'ROYAL TRAIN ON CAMDEN BANK'
by Gerald Broom GRA

The Coronation Scot

NEW STREAMLINED
RESTAURANT CAR EXPRESS

LONDON & GLASGOW IN 6½ HOURS

AVERAGE SPEED THROUGHOUT 61·7 M.P.H.

WEEK-DAYS *(SATURDAYS EXCEPTED)*

		P.M.			P.M.
LONDON (EUSTON)	dep.	1.30	GLASGOW (CENTRAL)	dep.	1.30
CARLISLE	arr.	6.13	CARLISLE	dep.	3.17
GLASGOW (CENTRAL)	arr.	8.0	LONDON (EUSTON)	arr.	8.0

Calls at Carlisle to set down passengers only. *Calls at Carlisle to pick up passengers only.*

Will not run on Friday, July 30th and Monday, August 2nd

THE NUMBER OF PASSENGERS IS LIMITED TO THE SEATING CAPACITY OF THE TRAIN AND SPECIAL RESERVATION TICKETS MUST BE HELD.

RESERVATION FEES First or Third Class for Single Journey 2/6

Seats should be reserved in advance at the following Offices :

LONDON *Enquiry Office, Euston Station or any Town Office, Suburban Station or principal Agency in London.*

GLASGOW *Enquiry Office, Central Station or any L M S Agency in Glasgow.*

CARLISLE *Station Master's Office.*

Orders for seats on this train can also be placed at any L M S Station, Town Office or Auxiliary Agency. In these cases passengers must apply for their Reservation Tickets at Euston or Glasgow Central Enquiry Offices before joining the train.

The first page in the LMS 1937 timetable was printed on a Coronation blue background.

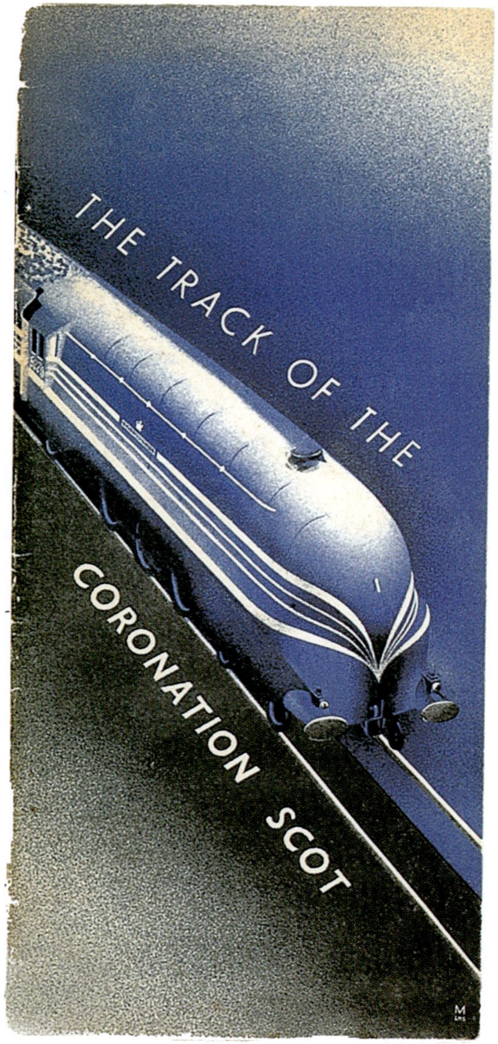

Front cover of the pamphlet The Track of The Coronation Scot *which contained some information about the train but mostly consisted of a detailed guide to the route.*

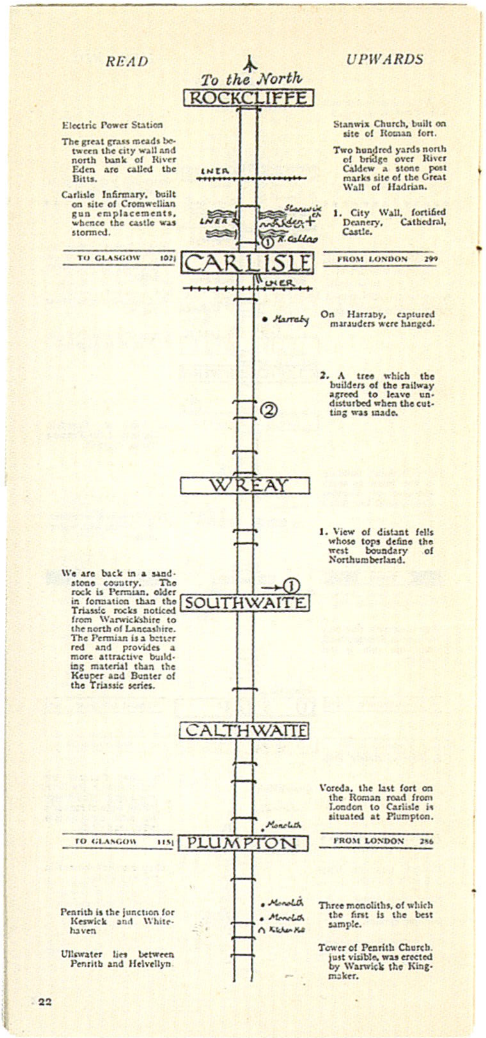
READ UPWARDS

To the North

ROCKCLIFFE

Electric Power Station

The great grass meads between the city wall and north bank of River Eden are called the Bitts.

Carlisle Infirmary, built on site of Cromwellian gun emplacements, whence the castle was stormed.

Stanwix Church, built on site of Roman fort.

Two hundred yards north of bridge over River Caldew a stone post marks site of the Great Wall of Hadrian.

1. City Wall, fortified Deanery, Cathedral, Castle.

TO GLASGOW 102¼ CARLISLE FROM LONDON 299

On Harraby, captured marauders were hanged.

2. A tree which the builders of the railway agreed to leave undisturbed when the cutting was made.

WREAY

1. View of distant fells whose tops define the west boundary of Northumberland.

We are back in a sandstone country. The rock is Permian, older in formation than the Triassic rocks noticed from Warwickshire to the north of Lancashire. The Permian is a better red and provides a more attractive building material than the Keuper and Bunter of the Triassic series.

SOUTHWAITE

CALTHWAITE

Voreda, the last fort on the Roman road from London to Carlisle is situated at Plumpton.

TO GLASGOW 115¼ PLUMPTON FROM LONDON 286

Penrith is the junction for Keswick and Whitehaven

Ullswater lies between Penrith and Helvellyn.

Three monoliths, of which the first is the best sample.

Tower of Penrith Church, just visible, was erected by Warwick the Kingmaker.

22

Specimen page from the route guide of The Track of The Coronation Scot.

'WINTER WAYFARERS'
by B. J. Freeman BA GRA

SOME FACTS ABOUT THE CORONATION SCOT

THE ENGINES

4-6-2 Streamlined Locomotives:
No. 6220 Coronation
No. 6221 Queen Elizabeth
No. 6222 Queen Mary
No. 6223 Princess Alice
No. 6224 Princess Alexandra

Boiler Pressure 250 lbs. sq. in.
Heating Surface 2807 sq. ft.
Superheater 856 sq. ft.
Total Weight, Engine and Tender, 164 tons 9 cwt.
Grate Area 50 sq. ft.
Cylinders (4) 16½″ × 28″
Coupled Wheels 6 ft. 9 ins.
Tractive effort 40,000 lbs.

THE TRAIN

Seating Capacity:
82 First Class; 150 Third Class
Total Weight 297 tons
The formation is as follows:
Corridor Third Class Brake
Third Class Vestibule Dining Car
Kitchen Car
Third Class Vestibule Dining Car
Third Class Vestibule Dining Car
Kitchen Car
First Class Vestibule Dining Car
Corridor First
Corridor First Class Brake

THE EUSTON HOTEL, LONDON, N.W.1., AND THE CENTRAL HOTEL, GLASGOW, ARE TWO OF THE 28 FAMOUS LMS HOTELS IN GREAT BRITAIN AND IRELAND

A menu from 'The Coronation Scot'.
Above left: *Front cover.* **Above right:** *Rear cover.* **Below:** *Contents.*

Luncheon

3/6

Crème Bretonne

—

Grilled Turbot Maitre d'Hôtel

—

Roast Beef Horseradish Sauce
Baked & Mashed Potatoes
Green Vegetables
or
Irish Stew

—

Pears Richelieu
or
Vanilla Ice

—

Biscuits Cheese Salad

—

Coffee, per Cup, 4d.

—

THIRD CLASS **AFTERNOON TEA, 1/3** 28/4/38. b

The LMS Official Time Table and the A. B. C. Railway Guide can be consulted and Writing Paper and Envelopes obtained on application to the Conductor.

In the general interest Passengers are requested to refrain from smoking immediately prior to and during the service of meals. Passengers are requested to see that their bills are written out in their presence, and not to pay any money until the bill has been presented.

Wines

		Bot. s. d.	½ Bot. s. d.
	CHAMPAGNE		
365	Perrier Jouët, Finest Extra Quality	17 6	9 6
318	Lanson, Extra Quality, Extra Dry ...	18 6	10 0
315	Veuve Clicquot, Dry...	19 6	10 6
351	G.H. Mumm, Cordon Rouge, Très Sec	19 6	10 6
345a	Geo. Goulet, Ex. Qual., Ex. Dry, 1928	21 0	11 0
	SPARKLING MUSCATEL		
259	"Golden Guinea"	15 0	8 0
	BORDEAUX RED		
30	Bordeaux Supérieur	4 0	2 0
31	Médoc	4 6	2 6
32	Margaux	6 0	3 6
	BORDEAUX WHITE		
52	Graves	4 0	2 0
252	Clos du Gravier, Extra Dry	4 6	2 6
54	Haut Sauternes	5 6	3 0
179	Graves Dry Royal, 1st Growth Podensac	7 0	4 0
185	Château Carbonnieux Château Bottled	10 0	5 6
	BURGUNDY RED		
56	Macon	5 0	2 6
59	Beaune	7 0	4 0
61	Pommard Supérieur, 1923	8 6	4 6
	BURGUNDY WHITE		
74	Chablis	5 0	3 0
	BRITISH EMPIRE WHITE		
762	South African Hock Type, Paarl Amber	5 0	3 0
757	Australian Highercombe Amber ...	6 0	3 6
760	South African, Dry Dominion Sparkling	12 6	7 0
	HOCK		
598	Laubenheim	5 0	3 0
615	Nierstein	7 6	4 0
603	Liebfraumilch	7 6	4 0
	MOSELLE		
599	Cueser-Berncasteler	5 0	3 0
661	Zeltinger	7 0	4 0
	SHERRY		
4	Amontillado, Pale Dry *per glass*	1/-	
1	Fine Rich ... ... ,, ,,	1/-	
	PORT		
15	Ruby ... ... ,, ,,	1/-	
400	Vintage Character ... ,, ,,	1/6	5 0
401	Finest Old Tawny ... ,, ,,	1/6	5 0

		s. d.
	GORDON'S "SHAKER-BOTTLE" COCKTAILS	
	Bronx, Dry Martini, Martini, Manhattan Piccadilly, ...	1 6
	WHISKY	
138	"ROYAL SCOT" finest procurable	- 10
	Other Proprietary Brands	1 0
	GIN	
	Booth's Old Matured Dry	1 0
	Finest Unsweetened	- 10
	Gin and Bitters	1 0
	Gin and Vermouth	1 0
	Vermouth French or Italian	1 0
	COGNAC	
	Fine Old Cognac	1 6
		liqueur glass
134	Cognac Vieux Maison, 40 years old	1 6
207	Hine's Grande Champagne, 25 years old ...	2 0
	LIQUEURS, &C.	
	Drambuie "Scotland's Own Liqueur" ...	1 0
	Crème de Menthe; Curaçao; Cherry Brandy	1 0
	Kümmel; Bénédictine; Grand Marnier ...	1 6
	Cointreau	1 6
	BEER, CIDER, AERATED WATERS, &C.	
	Bass' No. 1 Barley Wine ... *per nip*	1 0
	Bass' or Worthington's Pale Ale, *per bottle*	- 11
	Guinness' Stout	- 11
	Graham's Golden Lager	- 11
	"Red Tower" Lager	- 11
	Barclay's "London" Lager	- 11
	Pilsner Urquell	1 6
	Cider	1 0
	Bulmer's "Pomagne" per bot. 4/-, *per ½ bot.*	2 6
	Ross's The Belfast Ginger Ale *per bottle*	- 8
	Schweppes' Sparkling Grape Fruit	- 8
	,, Sparkling Lime	- 8
	,, Aerated Waters	- 8
	,, Soda Water ... *small bottle*	- 5
	Sparkling Buxton ... *per bottle*, 8d., *split*	- 5
	Apollinaris ... ... *per bottle* 1/-, *split*	- 6
	Perrier ... ... 1/-, ,,	- 6
	Still Malvern ... ... *per bottle*	- 8
	Vichy Celestins	1 6

QUARTER BOTTLES

CHAMPAGNE G. H. Mumm, Cordon Rouge, 5/-

OTHER WINES

Bordeaux Supérieur 1/- - Graves 1/- - Haut Sauternes 1/6 - Hock 1/6
Moselle 1/6 - Macon 1/6 - Chablis 1/6
Sherry No. 1 & 4 2/6 Port No. 400 & 401 2/6

LIGHT REFRESHMENTS AVAILABLE WHEN TABLE D'HOTE MEALS ARE NOT BEING SERVED

Tea or Coffee, 2 Poached or Boiled Eggs, Bread and Butter, &c.	2 6
Tea or Coffee, Fish or Plate of Cold Meat, Salad, &c.	3 6
Meat Sandwiches ... *each* – 6 Glass of Hot or Cold Milk	– 3

It will be appreciated if patrons will report any unusual service or attention on the part of Dining Car Attendants to Arthur Towle, Controller, LMS Hotel Services, St. Pancras Chambers, Euston Road, London, N.W.1. This will enable the management to recognize exceptional efficiency, which they desire to encourage in their services

'CORONATION SCOT PASSING STANDISH, 1937'
by Gerald Broom GRA

Above: *Front and rear covers of the pamphlet on 'The Coronation Scot' produced for the New York World's Fair in 1939.*
Below: *The pamphlet mainly contained information on railways in Britain, the train and the country through which it passed. This section also contained a message from Lord Stamp.*
Left: *After the start of the Second World War, a slightly more 'economy' version of the pamphlet was produced for the World's Fair in 1940, The text was changed to give some information about the war effort, and the message from Lord Stamp was revised accordingly.*

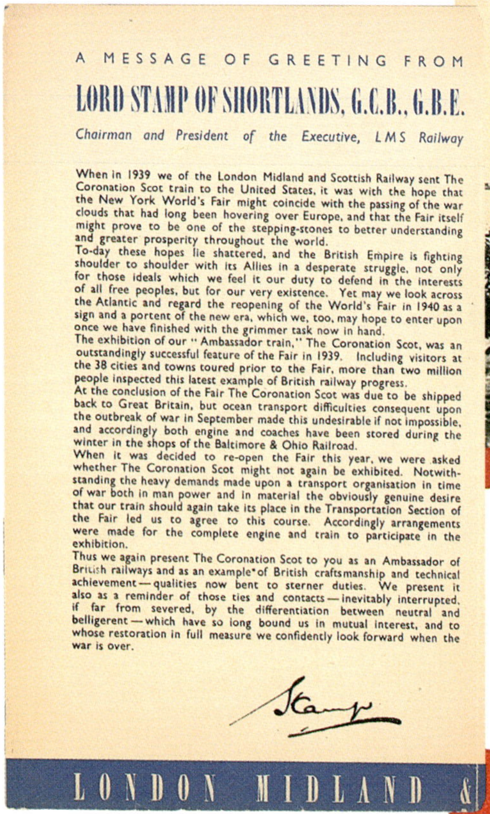

A MESSAGE OF GREETING FROM

LORD STAMP OF SHORTLANDS, G.C.B., G.B.E.

Chairman and President of the Executive, LMS Railway

When in 1939 we of the London Midland and Scottish Railway sent The Coronation Scot train to the United States, it was with the hope that the New York World's Fair might coincide with the passing of the war clouds that had long been hovering over Europe, and that the Fair itself might prove to be one of the stepping-stones to better understanding and greater prosperity throughout the world.

To-day these hopes lie shattered, and the British Empire is fighting shoulder to shoulder with its Allies in a desperate struggle, not only for those ideals which we feel it our duty to defend in the interests of all free peoples, but for our very existence. Yet may we look across the Atlantic and regard the reopening of the World's Fair in 1940 as a sign and a portent of the new era, which we, too, may hope to enter upon once we have finished with the grimmer task now in hand.

The exhibition of our " Ambassador train," The Coronation Scot, was an outstandingly successful feature of the Fair in 1939. Including visitors at the 38 cities and towns toured prior to the Fair, more than two million people inspected this latest example of British railway progress.

At the conclusion of the Fair The Coronation Scot was due to be shipped back to Great Britain, but ocean transport difficulties consequent upon the outbreak of war in September made this undesirable if not impossible, and accordingly both engine and coaches have been stored during the winter in the shops of the Baltimore & Ohio Railroad.

When it was decided to re-open the Fair this year, we were asked whether The Coronation Scot might not again be exhibited. Notwithstanding the heavy demands made upon a transport organisation in time of war both in man power and in material the obviously genuine desire that our train should again take its place in the Transportation Section of the Fair led us to agree to this course. Accordingly arrangements were made for the complete engine and train to participate in the exhibition.

Thus we again present The Coronation Scot to you as an Ambassador of British railways and as an example of British craftsmanship and technical achievement—qualities now bent to sterner duties. We present it also as a reminder of those ties and contacts—inevitably interrupted, if far from severed, by the differentiation between neutral and belligerent—which have so long bound us in mutual interest, and to whose restoration in full measure we confidently look forward when the war is over.

Stamp

LONDON MIDLAND &

TYPICAL SCOTTISH SCENERY

1. OBAN, renowned Scottish seaside resort surrounded by the Scottish mountains and overlooking a loch studded with islands, is reached over an entrancingly beautiful section of track from Glasgow (117 miles).

•

2. EDINBURGH, Scotland's capital (400 miles from London), is full of memories of Sir Walter Scott and Robbie Burns, as well as of the remote past. It is Scottish to the core, and one of the most beautiful cities of the world. From here you can take the famous one-day trip through the Trossachs.

•

3. LOCH LOMOND (THE TROSSACHS TOUR). All visitors from overseas include the Trossachs Tour from Edinburgh or Glasgow in their itinerary. It lies through the country of The Chase in Sir Walter Scott's "Lady of the Lake" and provides in one day all the glories of the Highlands—heather-clad hills, shimmering lochs, colourful forests, and rugged majestic mountains.

•

4. GLENEAGLES HOTEL stands for golf — super-golf on three courses which are the last word in construction. The hotel itself, run by the L M S, is a sports resort of international importance, one of the wonder-hotels of Europe. The L M S Company have other luxury hotels in Scotland at Edinburgh, Glasgow, Turnberry, Kyle of Lochalsh and Strathpeffer.

A MESSAGE OF GREETING FROM

LORD STAMP OF SHORTLANDS, G.C.B., G.B.E.

CHAIRMAN AND PRESIDENT OF THE EXECUTIVE, LMS RAILWAY

WHY are we sending the Coronation Scot train to America ?

In 1933 we sent you an Ambassador of goodwill and technical achievement, the Royal Scot train. You responded magnificently and the train was crowded wherever it stopped, from morn till night. Millions went miles just to watch her go by. New as tomorrow, it yet made thousands feel a touch with the Old Country.

The Royal Scot made many friends for Great Britain, for those Officers of my Company who were associated with the venture, and for myself.

The Coronation Scot, which comes to you as the latest product of the science of British Railroading, comes then as a cementer of these friendships. It will make a tour of the United States, and be our exhibit at the World's Fair in New York, where we of the London Midland & Scottish Railway feel that we are providing a representative worthy of this important occasion. We believe, too, that the Coronation Scot provides visible evidence of the advance that has been made in Great Britain in railroad transportation since the Royal Scot visited you six years ago.

May we also hope that the visit of the Coronation Scot can have an even wider significance than mere commercial objects ? There is nobody in Great Britain who does not admire the courage and foresight shown in organizing the New York World's Fair at a time when trade has been receding and when the world outlook is not wholly peaceful. Yet, just as in 1933, the visit of the Royal Scot preceded a revival in business and industrial activity on both sides of the Atlantic, so may we hope the World's Fair and this new tour of an L M S train will coincide with a new period of peace and prosperity for both our nations.

Stamp

'CORONATION SCOT ON DILLICAR TROUGHS'
by Gerald Broom GRA

'DAYS OF RED AND GOLD'
by B. J. Freeman BA GRA

Plate 68: *No. 6227* Duchess of Devonshire *at Polmadie shed, Glasgow, in the company of a former Caledonian Railway engine on the left and a 'Jubilee' on the right.*
Courtesy D. R. Bell

Plate 69: *No. 6226* Duchess of Norfolk *in the bay at the north end of the main down platform at Crewe on 3rd June 1938. A slight difference in the second batch is very noticeable in this picture, the three vents in the casing ahead of the cylinders. One of the streamlined lamps is in the 'top of the smokebox' position.* E. R. Morten

Plate 70: *An unusual rear view of No. 6226* Duchess of Norfolk *taken on the same occasion as the previous picture and showing the top of the engine and tender as it pulls away to the north.*
E. R. Morten

Plate 71: *No. 6228* Duchess of Rutland *taking water at Shrewsbury on the usual fill-in turn before returning to Crewe.*
A. G. Ellis collection

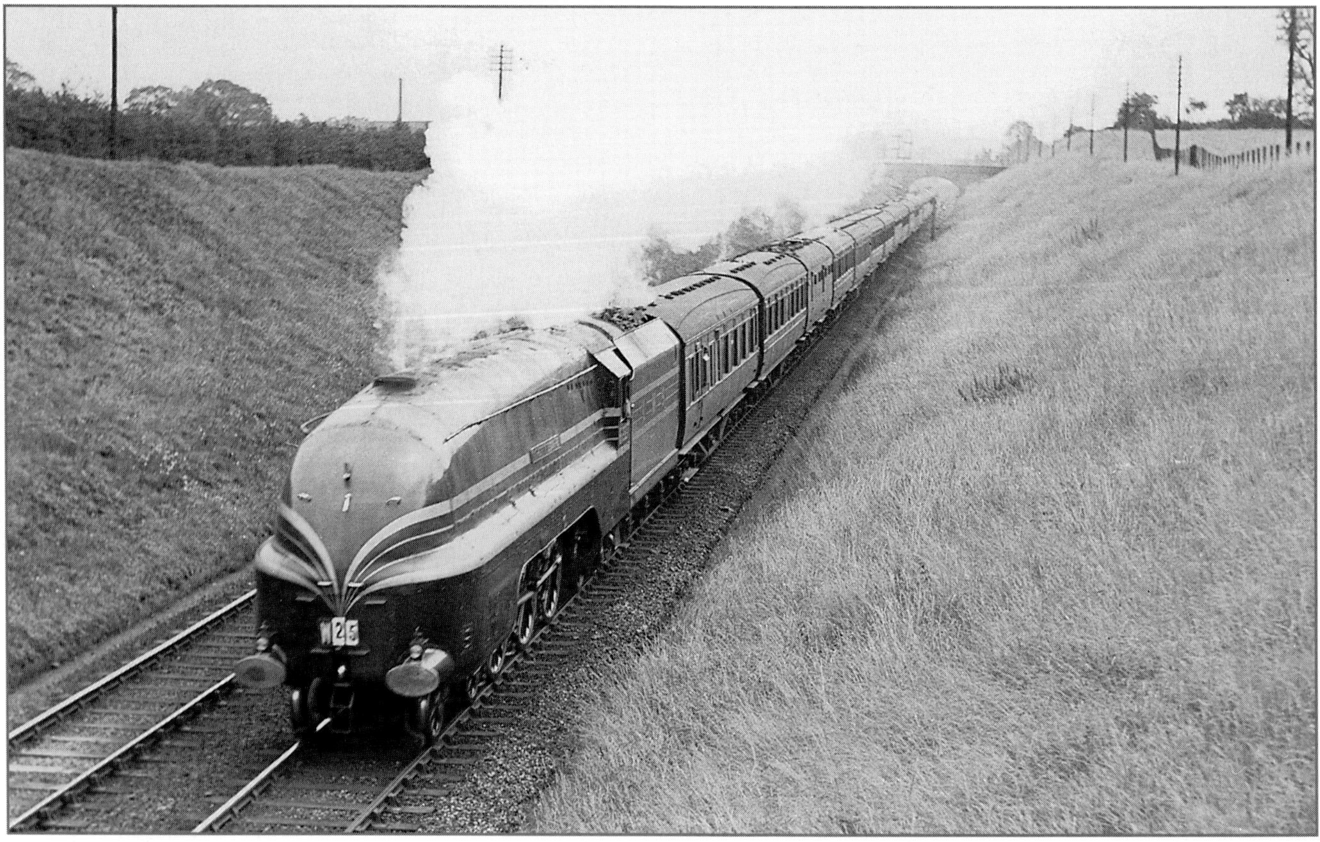

Plate 72: *No. 6227* Duchess of Devonshire *south of Lichfield with an up express loaded to 15 or 16 coaches on 16th July 1938.*
E. R. Morten

tuations in the blast, variations in the height and shape of the coal surface in the tender and between the relative heights of engine and tender as supplies of coal and water in the latter were used up. But the report concluded that a lip about one inch high 'should be able to prevent draughts into the cab'. In fact the investigations showed that the desired result could be achieved without any partial cover over the tender at all, by arranging for the top of the forward bulkhead of the tender to project an inch or two above the level of the flexible hood which extended between the tender and the cab roof.

Nevertheless, the eventual solution adopted was to fit a partial cover over the front part of the tender shaped as if it were an extension of the cab roof with a lip at its rear end. This cover left an opening 11ft 7¾in long over the coal space. The first five engines of course entered service without it but it was fitted quite soon, probably later in 1937, and it became a feature of all streamlined engines built subsequently.

Coal Consumption

In the middle of 1938 further 'Coronation' class Pacifics were built at Crewe. Five of them were streamlined, Nos 6225-9; they had the same livery scheme as the first batch but in standard LMS maroon and gold instead of blue and silver. The next five were non-streamlined, Nos 6230-4, and were painted in the standard maroon of the day. All were named after 'duchesses', thus perpetuating the theme of the first five in honouring female personages among the nobility.

When these new engines were in service, some effort was made to investigate their coal consumption. It was generally accepted that streamlining produced a worthwhile reduction and this belief had the support of the wind tunnel tests. After the first streamlined engines entered service, however, no attempt was made to verify the findings in practice or to quantify the saving. The only attempt to do so appears to have been a comparative study carried out by the Research Department, Derby, in the middle of 1938 and described in its report dated 25th October 1938. Two groups of engines, four streamlined, Nos. 6225-8, and five non-streamlined, Nos. 6230-4, worked four Camden jobs for eight weeks in August and September, each group working each job for four weeks. Their coal consumption was recorded on the basis of the weight of coal delivered to the engines by the coaling plants at the various sheds.

The report began by predicting the saving due to streamlining. Its prediction was based on the results of the wind tunnel tests and on a value of 1.622lb of coal per indicated horse-power hour. This figure was supplied by the chief mechanical engineer's department and had been obtained during its tests of a 'Coronation' class engine. For simplicity the calculation was made on the assumption of 'still air' and was therefore conservative, since side winds on the whole increased the value of streamlining. Allowance was also made for the greater mechanical resistance of the streamlined engines due to their greater weight (the streamlined casing weighed 2.85 tons). The savings predicted on the basis of these calculations are set out in the table below:

Predicted Savings due to Streamlining

Camden Job No.	Service mileage in four weeks	Average speed in mph	Average Net Saving Horse-power	Coal lb/mile	Coal per four weeks, tons
2	22,470	54.9	43.2	1.275	12.79
3	19,260	50.2	32.3	1.043	8.97
4	22,470	45.9	23.9	0.844	8.46
5	22,470	44.2	21.0	0.770	7.72
Totals	88,670				37.94
'Coronation Scot'	16,050	61.78	62.8	1.65	11.82

The figures for 'The Coronation Scot' were equivalent to an annual saving of about 150 tons. This represented a greater saving than was predicted for Camden jobs 2-5 for three main reasons: the higher average speed of 'The Coronation Scot'; its lower weight; and its fewer stops on route.

Unfortunately, the figures obtained during the eight-week trials were incapable of providing verification of the predicted savings. The method of basing coal consumption on the records of the weight of coal delivered to the tenders at coaling plants was wildly inaccurate. These weights were 'frequently in error to very considerable extents' because they were taken from the jigger recorders, which were so inaccurate that it was the practice at the sheds to adjust the figures they gave over a period to agree with the weights of loaded coal wagons emptied into coaling plant hoppers.

Another reason was that spillage during coaling was greater with streamlined tenders than non-streamlined. Because of the front cover over the coal space, any coal which fell on to it was deflected on to the ground. Furthermore, the cover prevented the normal amount of coal from being carried at the front of the tender and so the men attempted to fill the rear higher to compensate, which again caused more to be spilt.

The report concluded that coal supplies to small groups of engines over an eight-week period varied between much wider limits than any coal saving due to streamlining. The problems of obtaining accurate figures were increased by two other factors. Firstly, the streamlined engines covered 'decidedly less' mileage than the other group. No. 6224, for example, made only three or four trips during each four-weekly period. Secondly, there were wide variations in coal consumption between different engines of the same group on the same job and between the same engine on different jobs, and these variations were much greater than any saving due to streamlining. One important reason for this seems to have been largely the inaccuracy of the basic information on coal consumed.

Finally, the report proposed various ways in which a

similar trial might be made more accurate in future, by weighing coal more accurately, extending the tests over a longer period, using the same number of engines in each group, and allowing for differences in weather and in the techniques of different crews. It suggested however that the simplest way of evaluating the advantages of streamlining would be to run two series of tests with the same engine, one with the streamlined casing and the other without. Unfortunately, a thorough investigation on these lines was never carried out.

Plate 73: *No.* 6227 Duchess of Devonshire *at Crewe about 1938. It is probably waiting to work the down 'Mid-day Scot', as the coach being added to the rear is GWR and is probably the through coach from Plymouth to Glasgow.*

Plate 74: *When not required for the 'Coronation Scot', the new streamlined engines worked other important expresses. Here , in 1938, an unidentified member of the class passes milepost 125, north of Rugeley Trent Valley, with the up 'Mid-day Scot' loaded to 15 coaches.* P. S. Kendrick

Chapter Three
'THE CORONATION SCOT' IN AMERICA

Though basically of standard LMS stock, the original 'Coronation Scot' train sets were excellent in themselves. The passenger accommodation had been considerably upgraded to provide superior comfort, design and finish, and the external livery was striking. Mechanically, the standard stock already had good riding characteristics and low wind resistance. Nevertheless, in certain respects the LMS high-speed train sets compared unfavourably with those produced by the LNER at Doncaster for its 'Coronation'.

The LNER had set out to design a new train specifically for high-speed running. To minimise weight, for example, the eight-coach train sets employed articulation and so were made up of four articulated twin sets, while to reduce air resistance rubber sheeting was used to cover the gap between adjacent coach ends so as to maintain a continuous line, and valances were fitted under the coaches to fill the gap between the bogies. Internally the difference was less marked and was more a matter of taste, though without doubt the LNER train provided spacious accommodation in distinctive surroundings and had the advantage of enabling all passengers to take meals at their seats.

There is no evidence, however, that the LMS authorities decided to build a better train because they felt the LNER train was superior, and it is possible that it was the intention originally to replace the 1937 trains. Perhaps the decision to mark the coronation of King George VI by the introduction of a high-speed Anglo-Scottish service was taken too late to design and build a completely new train. If so, modifying existing stock to provide the 1937 train would have saved time and allowed a purpose-built train to be produced later. On the other hand, there was enough time to produce a new design of locomotive.

All this, however, is entirely speculation. What is more certain is that the new train sets were planned quite soon after the original ones went into service if not

Plate 75 and 76: *The last of the second batch, No. 6229* Duchess of Hamilton, *was specially prepared while still under construction for 'The Coronation Scot' tour of the United States in 1939. These two views show the engine on first completion, posed alongside the Liverpool & Manchester Railway 0-4-2* Lion, *which was built 100 years previously, outside No. 10 Erecting Shop at Crewe Works on 25th August 1938.*

Plate 77: *No. 6229 entered traffic on 7th September 1938 in shop grey paint, rather than in the red and gold livery. This was the normal Crewe Works practice with class prototypes and engines that were exceptional in some way, such as those requiring a special finish for exhibition, and dated back at least as far as the early 1880s and probably to 1862. No. 6229 ran in that condition until it returned to Crewe Works later in the year to be specially prepared for display at the New York World Fair in 1939. The red livery was then applied and identities exchanged with No. 6220* Coronation. *It is seen here in shop grey at Crewe North shed on 25th September 1938.*

Plate 78: *No. 6229 leaving Shrewsbury with an express for Crewe in the autumn of 1938.*

before. At first the intention was to build three new trains for the summer services of 1940, but in 1938 an invitation was received to send an exhibit to the World's Fair in New York in 1939. Good contacts had already been established by the successful tour made by LMS 4-6-0 No. 6100 *Royal Scot* in North America in 1933. Thus when the American railroads were planning their contribution to the World's Fair and issued an invitation, they received a favourable response. Lord Stamp himself was convinced of the value of such visits. From the point of view of publicity alone they were an excellent investment since they attracted far more public interest than an equivalent sum spent on advertising. As new sets for 'The Coronation Scot' were already under consideration, it was eventually decided to build a complete train and send it to the fair.

The engine selected for the tour was the last of the second batch of five streamliners which were built at Crewe in the summer of 1938, No. 6229 *Duchess of Hamilton*. Even while under construction in the erect-

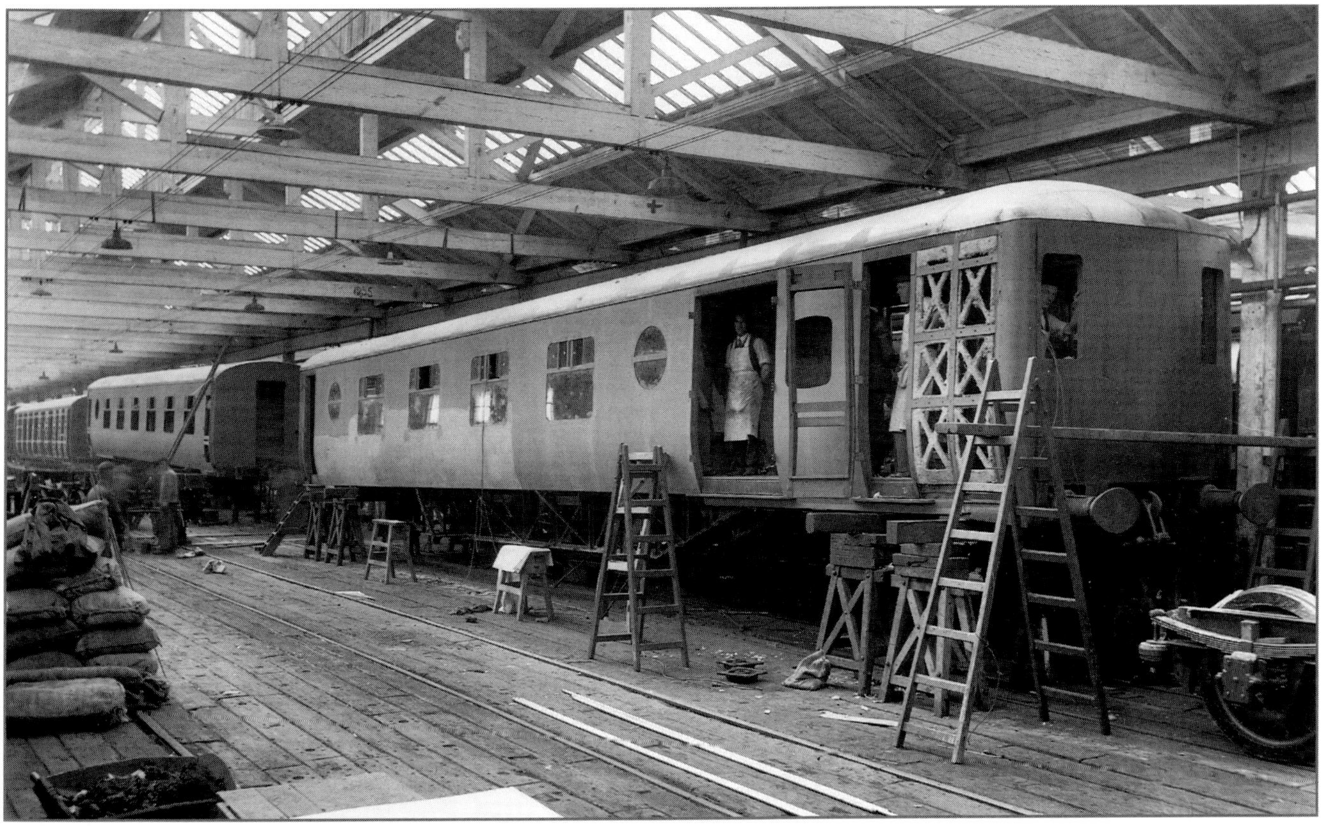

Plate 79: *Carriages for the 'Coronation Scot' tour of America under construction at Derby on 6th October 1938. Nearest the camera is corridor first brake No. 56000, which will be articulated to a corridor first and will be the leading vehicle in the train.*
National Railway Museum

ing shop, it was known to be destined for America, being generally referred to as the 'American engine', and as such it was given special treatment. It went into service in September in shop grey paint instead of the maroon and gold standard colours of the batch and was only painted fully after returning to the works for final preparation for the tour. As part of that process it was fitted with a bell and headlamp, and also exchanged identities with No. 6220 *Coronation* for the duration of the tour, swapping back again on return from the USA. This meant, of course, incidentally that the 'Coronation Scot' was hauled at times by No. 6229 *Duchess of Hamilton* in blue and silver.

The train which went to America in 1939 consisted of eight carriages in all, three articulated twin sets, a club saloon and a sleeping car. Only the articulated sets would normally have been part of the 'Coronation Scot' service. No place for the club saloon was envisaged in the plans for the 1940 'Coronation Scot' though clearly it could have been added to convey particularly important passengers if required. On the tour it fulfilled a very useful role in providing a suitable environment for entertaining visiting dignitaries. As the 'Coronation Scot' service operated in daytime there was no need for a sleeping car but it was included in the tour train as an example of a vehicle of its type and to provide emergency sleeping accommodation for staff during the tour.

In opting for articulation, the LMS designers were, of course, influenced by the need to save weight and were following the example set by the LNER. Indeed certain features of the LMS trains, such as the articulated couplings and the rubber sheeting between vehicles, followed Gresley articulated practice. Although the 1939 train never went into normal London-Glasgow service as 'The Coronation Scot', more vehicles of the types included in it were eventually built to provide three complete 'Coronation Scot' sets. The war delayed their construction and the last were only completed by BR as late as 1951.

The train was fully described in an official document produced by the Chief Mechanical and Electrical Engineer's Office at Euston and dated January 1939. It is typed on ordinary foolscap paper and has glued into it a number of actual prints from official photographs. It seems that it was not intended to be published or to be made available to the public directly but was compiled to be used as a hand-out to the press, particularly in the USA. Certainly an article which appeared in the American journal *Railway Age* on 1st April 1939 follows the text almost word for word. The description of the train which follows is taken from this official account:

"The American train is a portion of that under construction at the Derby Works of the LMS for service in Great Britain and consists of

Plate 80 (above): *The articulated gangway between a third diner and a kitchen car before the shrouding was placed in position.* National Railway Museum

Plate 81 (above right): *Shrouding in position between two articulated first-class vehicles.*
National Railway Museum

Plate 82 and 83: *Two views of an articulating bogie, 22nd November 1938.*
National Railway Museum

three articulated twin sets and two loose cars, made up as follows:

Corridor first brake)	Articulated twin set	
Corridor first)	16 & 24 seats	= 40 seats
Corridor first lounge)	Articulated twin set	
First-class dining car)	28 & 44 seats	= 72 seats
Kitchen car)	Articulated twin set	= 44 seats
Third-class dining car)		
First-class sleeping car	12 berths	
Club saloon	17 seats	
Totals:	173 seats and 12 berths	

'By the use of articulation the new train saves the equivalent in weight of roughly one coach. This can be seen from the following table comparing the weight of the vehicles in the train with that of similar vehicles of standard LMS construction.

	New Train			Older Stock		
	T	C	Q	T	C	Q
Corridor first brake) articulated	59	4	0	33	18	0
Corridor first)				36	8	0
Corridor first lounge) articulated	60	19	0	37	1	0
First-class dining car)				33	3	0
Kitchen car) articulated	66	18	3	39	9	0
Third-class dining car)				33	4	0
First-class sleeping car	44	0	0	44	0	0
Club saloon	31	8	1	32	10	0
Total	262	10	1	289	13	0

'The exterior painting follows the style of the earlier trains but the standard LMS crimson lake is used with gold bands instead of Coronation blue with silver bands. The four gold bands running the full length of the train continue round the shaped ends of the brake compartments at each end of the train and finish in a 'V' shaped point in the centre. As before, the gold bands on the engine also finish in a point on the centre of the smokebox.

'The exterior fittings of the carriages such as door handles and hinges are finished in satin matt nickel and the bodyside doors are fitted with spring-balanced frameless drop lights. In general, exterior projections are reduced to a minimum. The roofs, sides and ends are covered with 16swg steel panels finishing flush with the windows, and between the bogies is a sheet-metal valance to within 12in of rail level. To preserve continuity of line, the space between the adjoining ends of each pair of vehicles is closed with special rubber sheeting, fitted with an initial tension when in position. The exterior thus presents a smooth uniform appearance over the whole length of the train.

'Special attention has been paid to sound insulation. The corrugated steel floor sheets are welded to the steel underframes, and the underside of the sheets is sprayed with asbestos $^3/_8$in thick, while the flooring itself consists of cork 1$^5/_{16}$in thick on which is laid felt, linoleum and carpet. The inside of the roof, bodyside and end panels, and framework are also sprayed with asbestos, and the walls and partitions of the dining cars and the lounge car are lined with leather on a felt foundation. The bodysides are also fitted with twin glass windows having an air space of $^1/_4$in to insulate against heat and sound.

'Except for the sleeping car all the vehicles are of lightweight construction. The design of the body and underframe is arranged so that the solebars and cant rails form one unit and the trussed longitudinal members another. The solebars and cant rail are of high-tensile steel channel section, and welded to them are steel sockets to receive the teak body pillars which are bolted in position to the sockets. Between the quarter light pillars the body framing is reinforced by steel diaphragms which have steel angles spot-welded along each vertical edge. The diaphragms are welded to the solebar, cant rail and sockets, and attached to the timber pillars by bolts passing through the angles on the diaphragms. The latter have lightening spaces cut in them.

'The steel body panels, which are 16swg charcoal finish, are welded throughout in one unit extending between each pair of bodyside doors and secured in position by screwing to the timber framing and welding to the cant rail at the top. The 16swg galvanised steel roof panels are welded in position to the roof members, which are of light construction and secured to the cant rail by welding.

Ventilation of Body Framework

'The bodyside framework is ventilated throughout by introducing an air stream through grooves provided at regular intervals of 6in between the bottom edge of the bodyside steel panels and the timber securing fillets attached to the solebars. The steel roof panels are also arranged with the bottom edge clear of the bodyside panels, thus providing an air space along the whole length of the car. Complete circulation of air is effected by providing ventilation holes in suitable positions in the bodyside framing, cant rail and frame members. Extractor ventilators are fitted, evenly spaced, along the centre of the roof, in communication with the roof space for withdrawal of the circulating air.

Underframe and Bogies

All underframe members except for the solebars are of mild steel and welded throughout. At the outer end of each articulated underframe is fitted the standard draw and buffing gear and at the inner end the Gresley type of articulation coupling. The bogies are constructed of mild steel, welded throughout, and have concentric bolster and side laminated springs, following the design of those fitted on existing LMS articulated stock.

Decoration of First-Class Corridor Compartments

'The interior decoration of the corridor compartments is carried out on contemporary lines, a flush finish being obtained by the use of veneered panels. A variety of selected Empire timbers is used in conjunction with one of three colour schemes, blue-grey, brown and plum, each compartment being finished differently. The combinations of colour schemes and timbers used in the various vehicles are as follows:

Vehicle	Colour	Timber
Corridor first brake	Brown	Lacewood and beech
Corridor first brake	Plum	Australian maple and birch
Corridor first brake	Blue-grey	English willow
Corridor first brake	Brown	Walnut
Corridor first	Plum	Weathered sycamore and beech
Corridor first	Blue-grey	English willow
Corridor first	Brown	Planetree burr and beech
Corridor first	Blue-grey	Cherry mahogany (bleached) and Honduras mahogany
Corridor first	Plum	Walnut
Corridor first	Brown	Birch swirl and birch
Corridor first lounge	Plum	Australian maple and birch
Corridor first lounge	Blue-grey	Mountain ash and English ash
Corridor first lounge	Brown	Olive ash and English ash

'The corners of each compartment above the seats are rounded, with a cove veneered to match the panels, thus giving an unbroken line to the finish. Flush finished double sliding doors are fitted and the ceiling and walls above the cornice are finished with three-ply panelling ivory enamelled. The luxury seats, four in each compartment, are deep sprung with loose cushions and with Dunlopillo arm-rests and head-rests. They are upholstered in uncut moquette, self coloured except for vertical lines in the blending colours. Three colour schemes are used, blue grey, brown and plum, the curtains and carpets toning with each scheme. The cornice moulding and all other metal fittings are finished in satin matt brass. A telephone is fitted below each window for communication with the attendant in the kitchen car, and each passenger is provided with an electric cigar lighter.

'The corridors are also flush-finished, in figured teak with sycamore inlayed banding and walnut plinth. A carpet is provided to tone with the finishing timbers. The vestibules are spacious to facilitate the movement of passengers and have rounded corners at the body ends.

'The lavatory finish is in blue rexine with rounded corners and ivory ceiling, and the porcelain pedestal wash basin, lavatory hopper and toilet shelf are coloured to tone with the walls. Blue and white terrazzo mosaic is used for the floor, which is fitted with a deep cove to facilitate cleaning. Hot and cold water is provided and a 'Dixie' cup drinking machine with water filter is fitted. The windows in these compartments are circular, the top half being hinged for use as a ventilator.

Passenger Communication Apparatus

'The passenger communication apparatus, perhaps better known as the communication-cord apparatus, does not have the usual outside semaphores. Instead an indicator is fitted in the vestibules above the outside doors and in its normal running position shows a white disc behind a glass panel. When the apparatus has been operated, a red disc appears. It is returned to normal by the guard with a few turns of a key. This brings the white disc in view again and at the same time allows the valve to be reseated in the passenger communication valve box, which is situated on the end of the car and is connected to the vacuum brake train pipe in the standard manner.

The Dining Saloons

'In the interior decoration of the first and third-class dining saloons,

Plate 84: *Interior of a first-class compartment. The print over the seat depicts scenes on the Liverpool & Manchester Railway.*

a novel effect is obtained by lining the walls and partitions with leather on a felt foundation. The seats are also upholstered in leather and have loose cushions, the double seats being designed to give the passengers individual seating. The seat ends are also covered with leather and supported on two metal legs. All metal fittings are finished in silver-plated satin and the metal cornice mould has a leather insert coloured to tone with the walls of the saloon.

'The colour scheme for the first-class dining saloon is grey for the walls and seat ends with dull pink seats and backs, the sliding doors being faced with bakelite to match the walls. The third-class dining saloon has green walls and seat ends with brown for the seats and backs, and doors finished with bakelite panels. The ceilings in both saloons are panelled in three-ply with ivory enamelled finish. The fitted carpets and curtains are in colours to tone with the respective colour schemes.

'The seats are arranged two on one side of the gangway and one on the other, except at the doorways where there are only single seats on either side so as to provide ample space for the movement of passengers and attendants and avoid disturbing diners.

The Cocktail Lounge

'The interior decoration and arrangement of the cocktail lounge is distinctive and introduces some new features in railway carriage interior design. The walls do not follow the contour of the body side but are built out from the cant rail and provide a flat vertical side with wide window sills. The ventilating and heating duct is housed behind the bodyside panels, and an alcove electric light is fitted between each pair of windows and extends for their full depth. The curtains are so arranged as to hang back clear of the window span when not in use, giving the passengers full advantage of the large observation windows. This imparts a sense of spaciousness to the compartment.

'The walls and partitions are covered with blue leather mounted on felt, as in the dining cars, and are panelled out with chromium-plated mouldings. A portion of the ceiling across the car to the adjacent partitions is also covered with leather, leaving an ivory enamelled ceiling panel, down the centre of which runs a specially designed light fitting. The doors and sills are finished in blue bakelite.

'The colour scheme of the compartment is red, white and blue, the banquettes and fixed swivel chairs being upholstered in blue. The blue fitted carpet is divided into squares by red lines, and red and white are also used in the design of the curtains and table tops.

'The cocktail bar recess has a flat ceiling with a dome in which is placed a specially designed electric light fitting, and the walls adjoining the cocktail bar are covered with cream Wareite with interesting mural designs. The counter top is veneered with red blisterproof

Plate 86 (opposite upper): *General interior view of the first-class dining saloon.*

Plate 87 (opposite lower): *General interior view of the third-class dining saloon.*

Plate 85 (left): *Another first-class compartment, finished in English 'olive ash' and provided with a telephone.*

bakelite with stainless steel edgings. The front of the bar is padded with Dunlopillo rubber, which is covered with blue leather and divided horizontally into three sections with white leather-covered beads; it is finished with a stainless steel skirting. Spaced around the bar are three revolving stools upholstered in red leather and having chromium-plated tubular standards.

'The back of the bar is fitted out for service. A sink is provided with hot and cold water, the hot water being supplied from a boiler in the underframe below. Bottle racks and an ice refrigerator are also fitted, and a glazed screen with shelves is built into the vestibule partition, which is provided with a chromium-plated steel grille shutter on the bar side.

The Club Saloon

'The interior of the club saloon is finished in English brown oak, with ivory enamelled ceiling. The body side and partition panels are relieved by a triple twist rope moulding. Chairs and settees upholstered in coral vaumol hides are arranged in groups. The floor is covered with a nigger brown fitted carpet, divided into squares by red lines. The curtains are in colours to tone with the furnishings. An electric glow fire is fitted in the centre of the cross partition at the opposite end of the saloon to the brake compartment and with a settee and easy chairs suitably arranged gives a fireside effect to that end of the saloon.

Kitchen Car

'The kitchen car is well equipped for service on long journeys and has many new features. Special attention has been given to obtaining a hygienic finish and ensuring good ventilation for the car. The corridor is finished in bakelite, the lower panels being blue and the upper panels cream with a dividing line of red between them. The ceiling is in white bakelite and on the floor is blue and white Semtex flooring, to tone with the walls. The interior of the pantries, kitchen and staff compartment is lined with grey and white mottled bakelite panels with white bakelite ceilings.

'The kitchen equipment includes a solid fuel cooking range and boiler finished in black enamel and chromium plate. Water in the tea boiler and hot water supply tank above the cooking range is heated by steam coils fed from the steam boiler adjacent to the kitchen sinks. An ample supply of hot water for the sinks in each pantry and the kitchen is available. The hot plate cupboard alongside the cooking range is also heated by steam from the boiler. About 450 gallons of water are carried in the supply tanks.

'The coal fuel is supplied to the hearths by an automatic gravity feed. It is contained in hoppers fitted to the top of the boiler and cooking range. When in position each hopper is housed in an air-sealed chamber and is accessible from the corridor. Spare hoppers ready loaded with fuel are carried in a convenient position in the corridor and the process of replacing an empty hopper with a fully loaded one can be carried out quickly and easily. Hinged doors, which fold back level with the corridor partition, are fitted at the back of the cooking range and boiler. Each hopper contains about 28lb of fuel and is sealed by a removable bottom plate, which is not withdrawn until the hopper is in position. The fuel is thus not exposed to the atmosphere at any time and the risk of dust entering the car is thereby eliminat-

Plate 90: *View of fittings in the cocktail bar.*

Plate 88 (opposite upper): *The first-class lounge, looking towards the cocktail bar, in vehicle No. 56100. Again, the decor includes scenes on the Liverpool & Manchester Railway.*

Plate 89 (opposite lower): *The first-class lounge, looking away from the cocktail bar.*

Plate 91: *Corridor in the club saloon.*

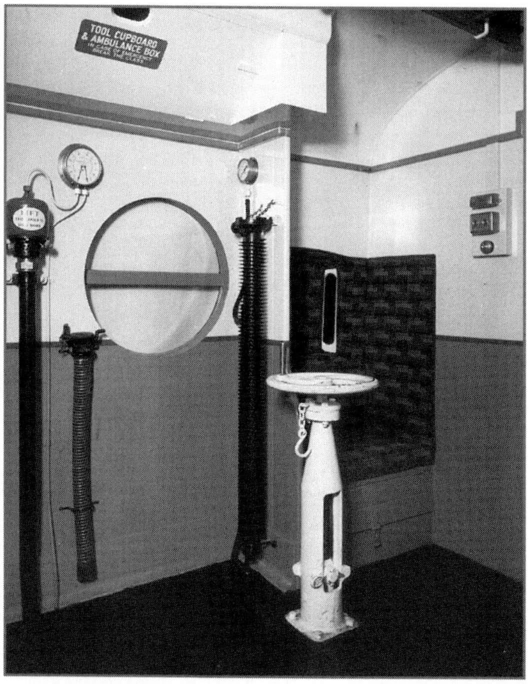

Plate 92 (far left): *The writing desk in one corner of the club saloon.*

Plate 93 (left): *The club saloon brake compartment.*

Plate 94 (below): *The club saloon.*

ed. Forced draught is used for the fires, the boiler and cooking range flues being connected with an electric fan at their junction. The steam pressure in the boiler is controlled by a thermostatically operated damper situated in the flue.

'The rest of the equipment in the kitchen and pantries is of the standard type used in LMS kitchen cars except for two of the refrigerators which are of the Frigidaire type.

Sleeping Car

'The sleeping car was built in 1936 and was withdrawn from traffic to accompany the train to America. It has a welded steel underframe and six-wheel bogies of the standard LMS design for this class of stock. The body framing consists of timber pillars secured by steel sockets which are welded to the underframe and steel angle cantrail. The body sides, ends and roof are covered with 16swg steel panels, which are welded to steel angle roofsticks.

'Twelve berths, lavatory and attendant's compartment are provided. The corridor is finished in walnut and sycamore. The walls of the berths are covered with blue green shaded rexine and the bedspreads and carpets are to tone. The wash basin is pale yellow porcelain with hot and cold water taps.

Electrical Equipment

'The electrical supply is provided by generators suspended from the carriage underframe and driven by belt from the axles. On the more heavily loaded coaches the generating sets are in duplicate. The equipment is of the Wolverton type, developed and patented by the LMS company, and manufactured in its own shops. Control of the generator, which is a plain shunt machine, is through the dynamo field by means of a variable contact resistance of carbon with step by step resistance units. Action is governed by a combination of coils which ensure an output in accordance with the requirements of the lighting and other loads in conjunction with appropriate battery charge. A single 12-cell battery is used with each equipment, manufactured by the Choride Electrical Storage Co Ltd. The cells are of the Exide-Ironclad type specially adapted for train lighting and giving a high capacity to weight ratio. To save weight, equipment components have been produced in aluminium wherever practicable. The lighting throughout the train is under the control of the guard. Light fittings are designed to conceal the source of the light.

'In the dining cars illumination is mainly indirect by means of fittings along the centre of the ceiling which project light on to it. The undersides of the fittings are in the form of a tray with louvred openings beneath each lamp, thereby permitting some direct but obscured light. Supplementary lighting for the dining tables is provided by lamps over each window.

'In the cocktail lounge alcove decorative wall panels supplement the lighting from a similar ceiling fitting. The bar is illuminated by a circular fitting of opal glass provided with metal louvres. In the club car there is a combination of circular ceiling fittings and wall brackets.

'The corridor compartments are illuminated by brackets in the standard position for local reading, with a fitting on the side wall over the entrance door for general lighting, the distribution from which is indirect. The brackets are so louvred that no direct light can strike the eyes of passengers and they can be individually switched. A dimming switch reduces the intensity of the general lighting for night travel. The mirrors of the lavatories have special fittings designed to give uni-

Plate 95: *Interior view of the kitchen car, showing the cooking ranges.*

Plate 96 (far left): *The pantry in the kitchen car.*

Plate 97 (left): *The telephone in the pantry of the kitchen car.*

form illumination without glare. The first-class compartments are provided with electric cigar lighters.

Heating

'Heating and ventilating are by means of Stone's Pressure Heating and Ventilating system. The equipment consists of a unit suspended on the underframe containing a motor-driven fan, a steam heating coil, motor-operated regulating gear, and primary and secondary air filters, the latter being of the viscous type. Control of temperature is automatic through the medium of a compensating thermostat panel, which maintains any pre-determined coach temperature over wide fluctuations of atmospheric temperature. The air is distributed throughout the coach by a system of ducting and is discharged at a very low velocity at floor level. Vents in the coach roof remove the air and are of such capacity that a light pressure is maintained within the coach whereby draughts are precluded. A complete air change is effected every five or six minutes. Special provision is made for rapid pre-heating of the coaches and for automatic stoppage of the circulating fan in the event of a failure of the steam supply during cold weather.

Sleeping Car

'In the first-class sleeping car, ventilation and heating are effected by Thermotank equipment. The ventilating unit is housed above the vestibule ceiling and supplies heated air and air at atmospheric temperature through separate ducts to a punkah louvre in each sleeping berth. The temperature of the air delivered to the berth can be regulated to the wishes of the individual passenger by adjusting the louvre. All the air is cleaned by filters of the viscous type. Ceiling, mirror and bed lights are provided, the latter having dimming facilities. Bell communication is available between each berth and the car attendant.

Communication

'Communication between the passenger compartments and the kitchen car pantries is by means of telephones. Each compartment has a hand-combination telephone recessed into the body side wall below the window. Depression of the key on the instrument lights a lamp and gives an audible call in the pantry to which the telephone is connected. The lamp indicates to the attendant the coach from which the call has originated. In the dining compartment and the club car, bell pushes are provided for the summoning of the dining car attendants.

'The kitchen car is provided with three refrigerated cabinets, one of which is devoted to wines. Cooling is by means of Frigidaire equipment operated from the train-lighting system. The same supply operates induced draught fans for the coal stove, a boiler feed pump and automatic damper control for the hot-water supply. On the lounge car there is a steam-electric water boiler for the provision of hot water to the sink of the cocktail bar. This boiler is thermostatically controlled on both forms of heating.'

List of Sub-contractors

Wheels and axles	Taylor Bros, Manchester
High tensile steel for underframe, solebar, and body cantrails	Colvilles Ltd, Glasgow
Mild steel for underframes bogies	Appleby Frodingham Iron & and Steel Co, Scunthorpe Dorman Long & Co Ltd, Middlesborough
Bogie concentric springs	Timmis Pilot Brand manufactured by Turton Bros &Matthews Ltd, Sheffield
Special bogie laminated auxiliary springs; buffing and drawbar springs	George Spencer Moulton & Co Ltd
Brake cylinders	The Vacuum Brake Co Ltd, London
Lighting system	Wolverton, LMSR
Lighting cells	Chloride Electrical Storage Co Ltd Clifton Junction
Heating & ventilating equipment	J. Stone & Co Ltd, Deptford Thermotank Ltd, Glasgow
Hot water boiler for cocktail bar	J. Stone & Co Ltd, Deptford
Auxiliary generating set	The General Electric Co Ltd, Birmingham
Body and roof exterior steel panelling	Smith and McLean Ltd, Glasgow
Dovetail sheeting	F. Braby & Co, Glasgow Lewis Construction Co Ltd, Hayes
Cork flooring for dovetail sheeting	J. W. Roberts, Ltd, Armley
Linoleum	Korkoid Decorative Floors, London
Carpets	T. F. Firth & Sons, Brighouse J. Templeton & Co Ltd, Glasgow
Insulating material for underside of floor and body walls and roof	J. W. Roberts & Co Ltd, Armley
Lavatory floors, terrazzo material	J. W. Roberts & Co Ltd, Armley
Kitchen corridor floor	Semtex Ltd, London
Glass	Pilkington Bros Ltd, St Helens Chance Bros & Co Ltd, Smethwick
Bodyside door droplights	Beckett Laycock and Watkinson Ltd, London
Sliding ventilator lights	Worcester Windshields and Casements Ltd, Worcester
Stepboard treads	Ferodo Ltd, Chapel-en-le-Frith
Roof ventilators, "Monsoon" type	Mead Maclean & Co Ltd, London
India-rubber gangway connections and valances for articulated ends of cars	George Spencer Moulton & Co Ltd London
Veneered finishing panels and partitions for corridors	Flexo Plywood Co Ltd, London Saro Laminated Wood Products Ltd, London
Finishing veneers for compartments	
Hides for walls of dining and lounge compartments	Connelly Bros Ltd, London
Hides for seats of dining compartments	- ditto -
Seat upholstery, corridor compartments	Edinburgh Weavers, Carlisle Old Bleach Linen Co Ltd, London
Curtains	Edinburgh Weavers, Carlisle
Rexine for lavatory walls and tables	Imperial Chemical Industries (Rexine) Ltd, Hyde
Lavatory water heaters	Westinghouse Brake and Signal Co Ltd, London
Lavatory porcelain hoppers and basins	Twyfords Ltd, Hanley
Seat and seat back springs	Lace Web Spring Co Ltd, Sandiacre
Special cushion fillings for head rest, arm rest and side elbows	Dunlop Rubber Co, Manchester
Cocktail bar and equipment	F. Sage & Co Ltd, London
Wareite decorative panels for cocktail bar	- ditto -
Furniture for lounge compartment	- ditto -
Furniture for club saloon	Waring & Gillows Ltd, London
Electric light fittings	The General Electric Co Ltd, Birmingham
Telephones	
Cigar lighters	S. Smith & Sons Ltd, Cricklewood
Refrigerator for kitchen car	Frigidaire Ltd, London
Bakelite panelling for kitchen car	Bakelite Ltd, Birmingham Flexo Plywood & Co Ltd, London
Brass mouldings for interior finish	Jones & Foster Ltd, Birmingham Metal Mouldings Ltd, London
Cooking range and boiler	British Coal Utilisation Research Association, manufactured by Wm Green & Co (Ecclesfield) Ltd, Sheffield
Locks and handles	J. & E. Bates & Son, Wolverhampton J. Kaye & Sons, Leeds N. F. Ramsay & Co, Birmingham Yale & Towne Ltd, Willenhall
Ball bearings for sliding door gear	Skefko Ball Bearings Co Ltd, Luton
Paint	Docker Bros, Birmingham
Sleeping car bed linen and seat antimacassars	Belfast Linen

Plate 98: *Rear view of the train which was sent to America. The gold stripes came to a point on the end of saloon No. 823 and so complemented the style of the front of the engine.*

Plate 99: *View of the front of the train taken on the same occasion, with articulated twin carriages Nos 56000 and 56001, corridor brake first and corridor first, nearest the camera.* National Railway Museum

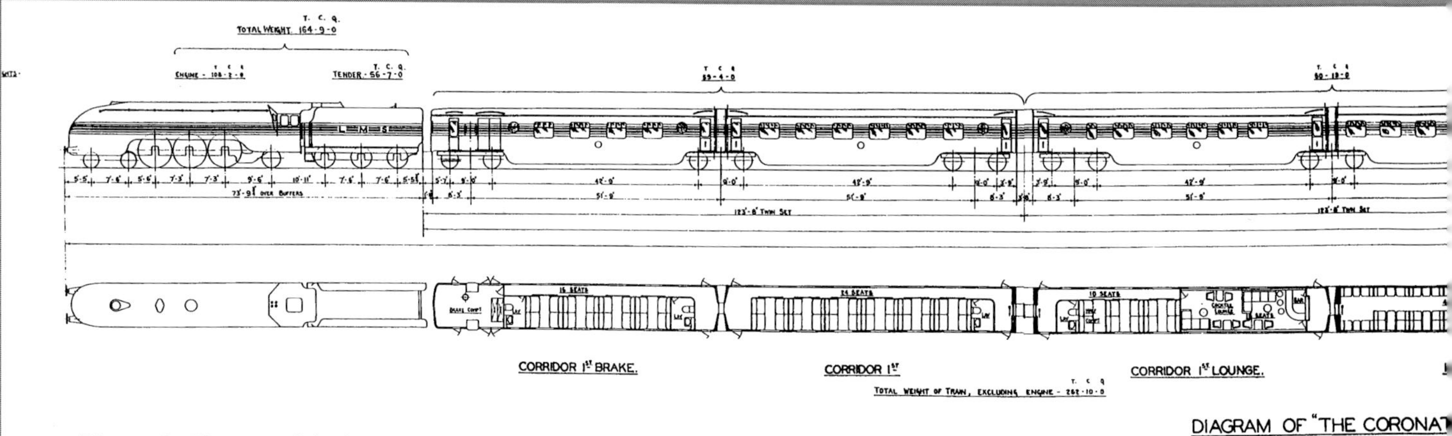

Figure 6: *Diagram of the 'Coronation Scot' train for America, taken from the official booklet..*

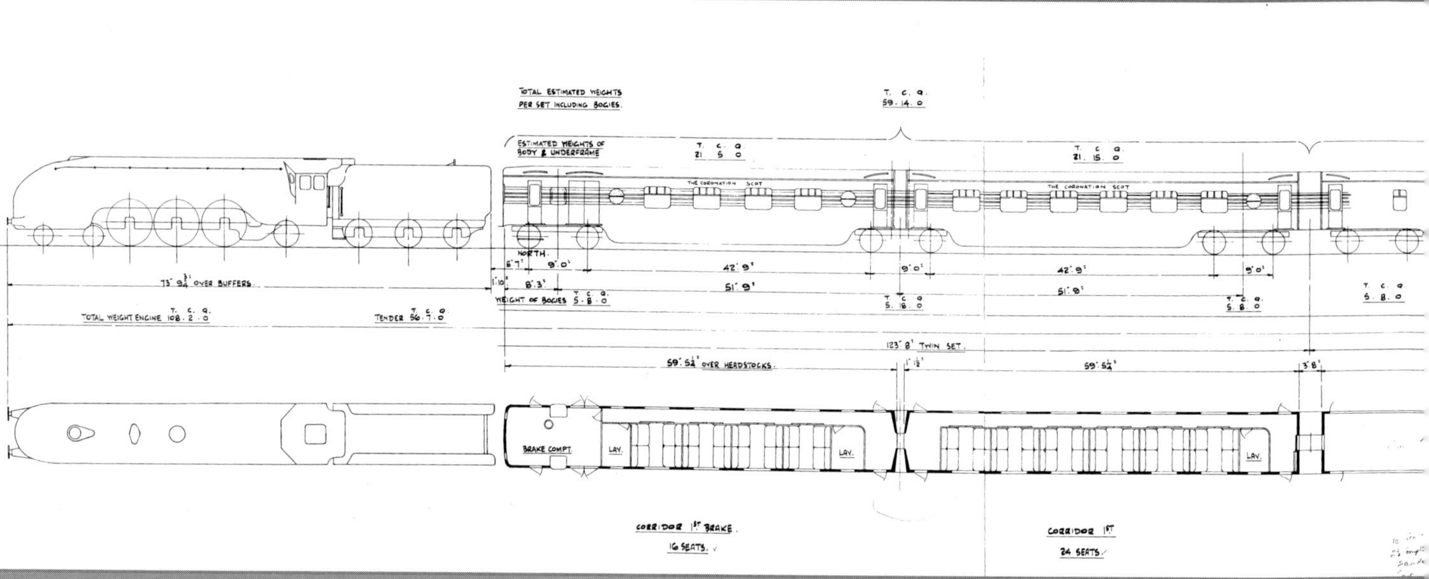

Figure 7: *Diagram of the new train planned for the 'Coronation Scot' service in 1939 and signed by W. A. Stanier himself. It is described as the 'English' train , to distinguish it from the train sent to America.*
Courtesy Michael Brooks

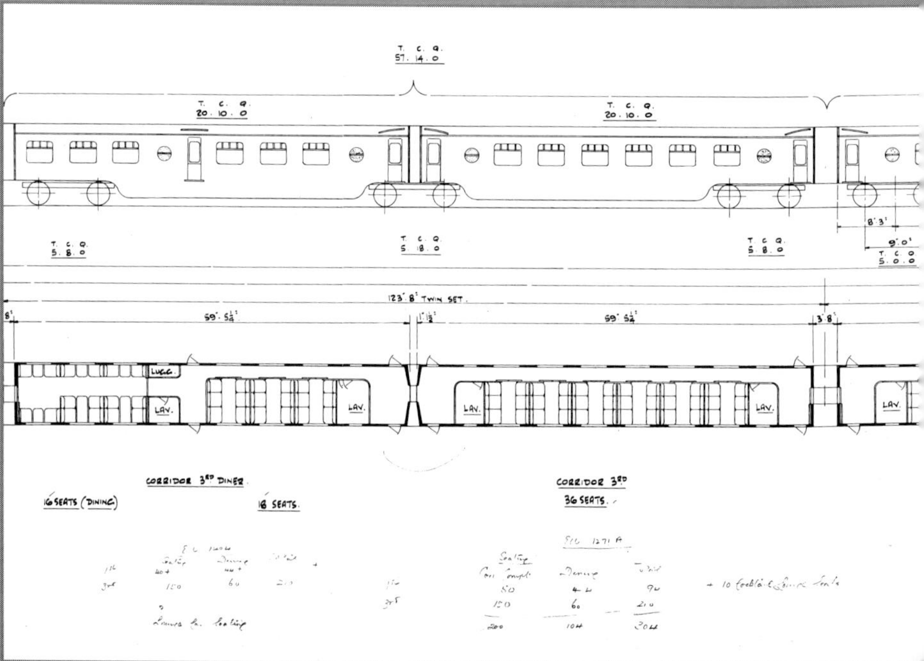

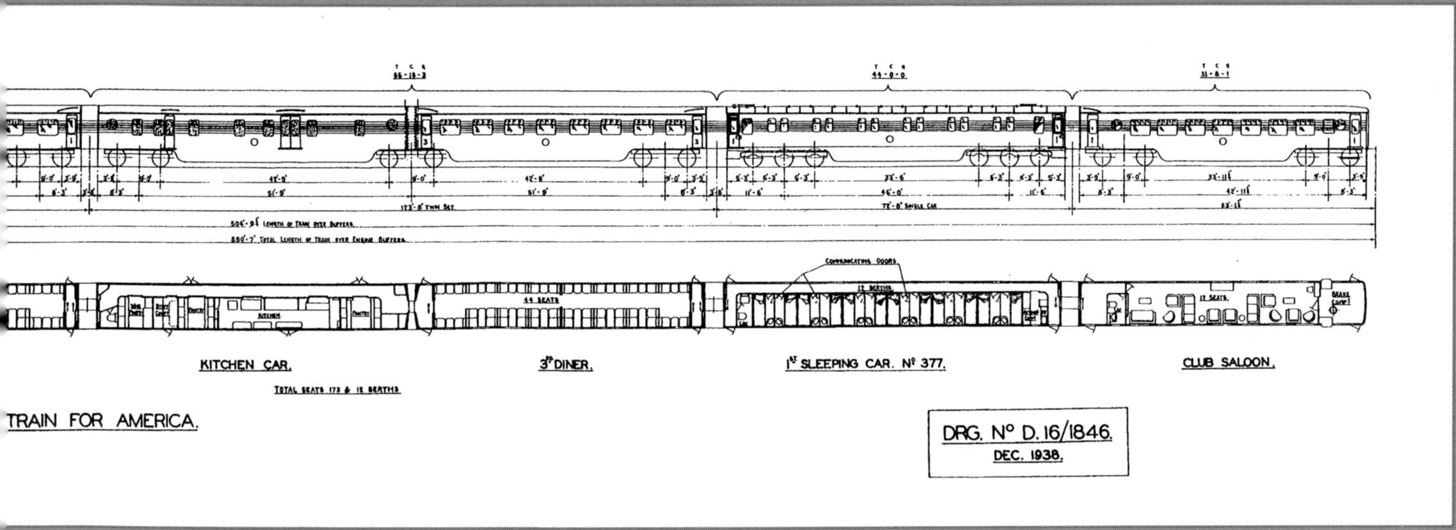
T C Q
44-0-0
T C Q
31-8-1
COMMUNICATING DOORS
44 SEATS
12 BERTHS
17 SEATS
BRAKE COMPT
KITCHEN
PANTRY
KITCHEN CAR.
3RD DINER.
1ST SLEEPING CAR. No 377.
CLUB SALOON.
123'-8" TWIN SET
73'-8" SINGLE CAR
TOTAL SEATS 173 & 12 BERTHS
TRAIN FOR AMERICA.
DRG. No D.16/1846.
DEC. 1938.

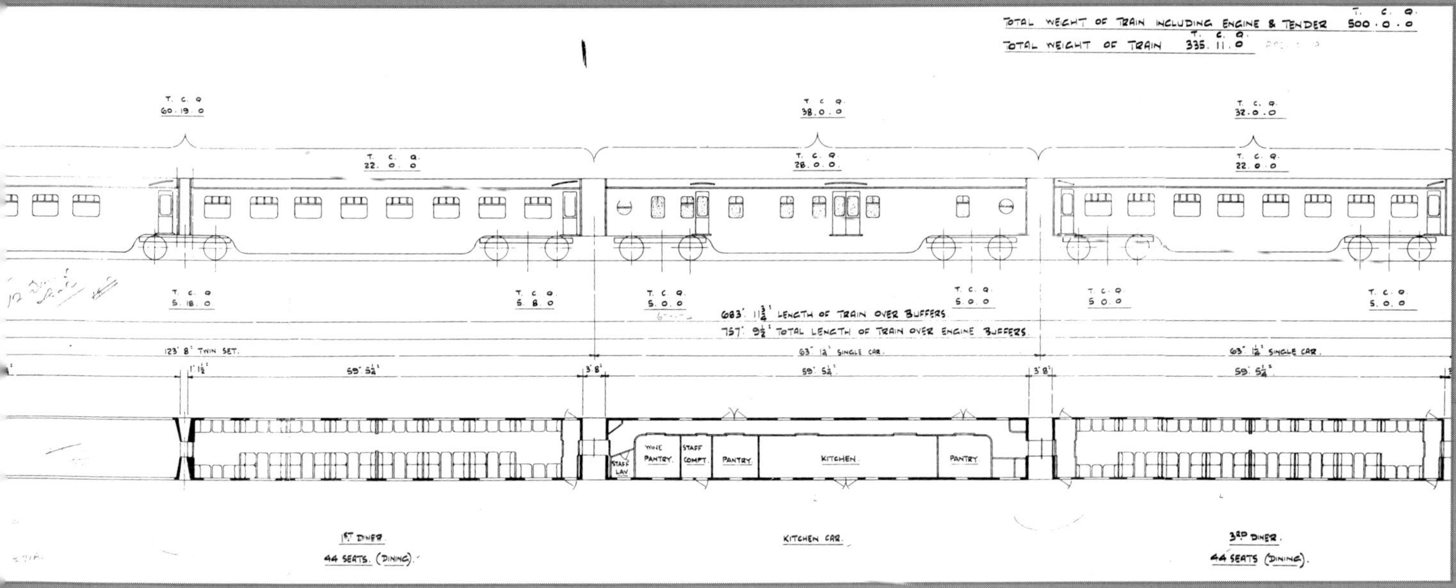
TOTAL WEIGHT OF TRAIN INCLUDING ENGINE & TENDER T. C. Q. 500.0.0
TOTAL WEIGHT OF TRAIN T. C. Q. 335. 11. 0
T. C. Q.
60. 19. 0
T. C. Q.
38. 0. 0
T. C. Q.
32. 0. 0
T. C. Q.
22. 0. 0
T. C. Q.
28. 0. 0
T. C. Q.
22. 0. 0
T. C. Q.
5. 18. 0
T. C. Q.
5. 8. 0
T. C. Q.
5. 0. 0
T. C. Q.
5. 0. 0
T. C. Q.
5. 0. 0
T. C. Q.
5. 0. 0
683' 11¾" LENGTH OF TRAIN OVER BUFFERS
757' 9¾" TOTAL LENGTH OF TRAIN OVER ENGINE BUFFERS
123' 8" TWIN SET.
63' 1½" SINGLE CAR.
63' 1½" SINGLE CAR.
1' 1½"
59' 5¼"
3' 8"
59' 5¼"
3' 8"
59' 5¼"
WINE PANTRY.
STAFF COMPT.
STAFF LAV.
PANTRY.
KITCHEN.
PANTRY.
1ST DINER
44 SEATS. (DINING).
KITCHEN CAR.
3RD DINER.
44 SEATS (DINING).

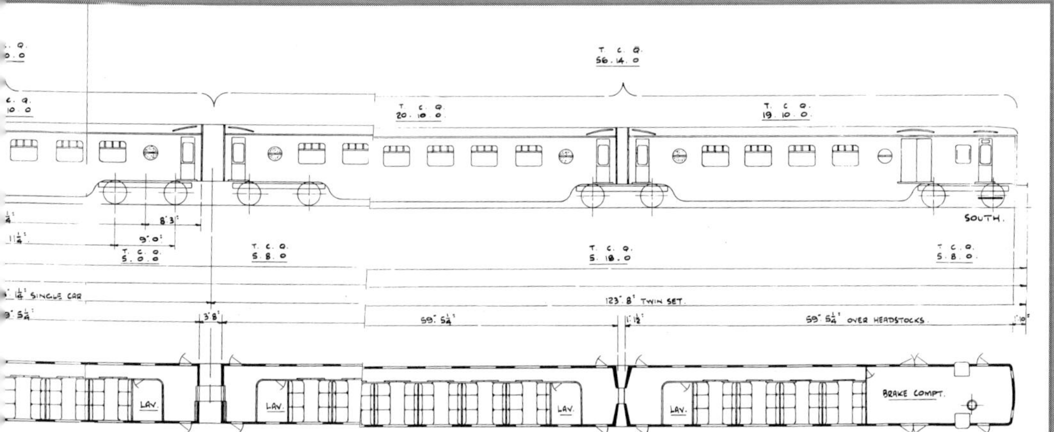
T. C. Q.
56. 14. 0
T. C. Q.
20. 10. 0
T. C. Q.
19. 10. 0
SOUTH.
8' 3"
9' 0"
T. C. Q.
5. 0. 0
T. C. Q.
5. 8. 0
T. C. Q.
5. 18. 0
T. C. Q.
5. 8. 0
1½" SINGLE CAR
123' 8" TWIN SET.
3' 8"
59' 5¼"
1' 1½"
59' 5¼" OVER HEADSTOCKS.
LAV.
LAV.
LAV.
LAV.
BRAKE COMPT.
CORRIDOR 3RD
36 SEATS.
CORRIDOR 3RD BRAKE
24 SEATS.
— ARTICULATED CORONATION SCOT. — DIAGRAM OF TRAIN. —
(FORMATION OF ENGLISH TRAIN).
CME. EUSTON. JAN. 1939. SCALE ⅛" : 1 FOOT.
W A Stanier
16-1-39.

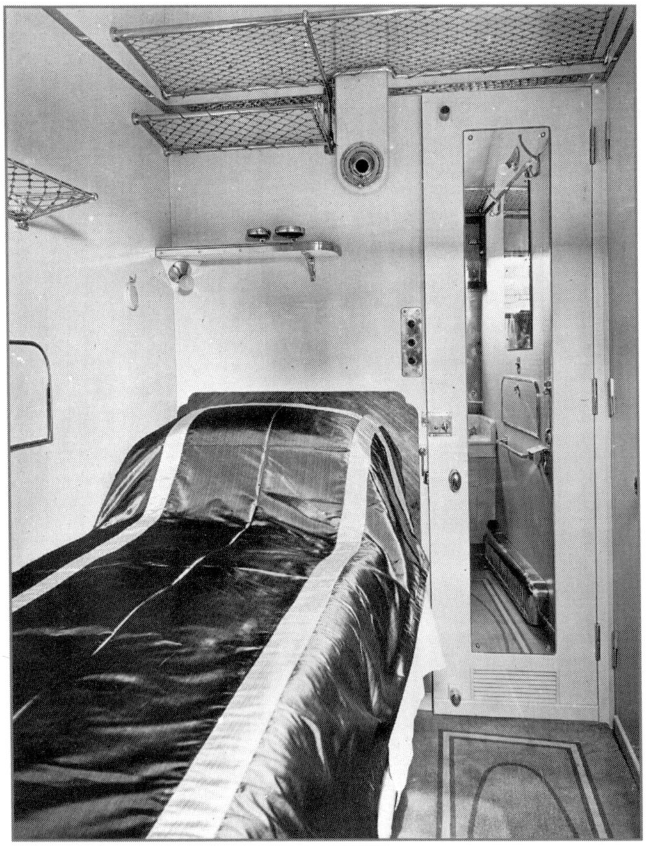

Plate 100: *A berth in the first-class sleeping car.*

The American Tour

Before the departure of 'The Coronation Scot' on its tour of America the engine and train were put on show to the public for a few days at Euston. An official luncheon was held there on 9th January 1939 to bid the train farewell. Among the guests was a small number of the company's employees from Crewe and Derby Works. They were invited as representatives of those who had built the engine and train. Lord Stamp himself wished the select team of four men who were to work on the train *bon voyage*. In charge of the tour was Robert A. Riddles, who was then Mechanical and Electrical Engineer, Scotland; the train fitter was F. W. Soden, an assistant erecting shop foreman at Crewe Works; and the engine crew were Driver Fred C. Bishop and Fireman John McKinnon Carswell, both of Camden. The plan was for the train to make a 3121-mile tour and then be exhibited at the World's Fair in New York.

Ten days later, on 19th January, the locomotive and train were hauled to Southampton where on the following day they were loaded on to the M. S. *Belpamela*, a Norwegian freighter belonging to the Christen Smith line. A special track had already been laid down on the quayside and tested by a Southern Railway 'Lord Nelson' class 4-6-0. Complaints were made in the press about the use of a foreign-owned ship to convey such a prestigious British train on such an important occasion. The 'Bel' ships of the Christen Smith line, however, were specially designed to carry railway equipment. The ship itself had a 150-ton derrick and so could load and unload at ports which were not equipped with suitable cranes. With this equipment the engine, tender and one carriage were stowed in the hold and the rest of the carriages, protected by thick wax, were carried on the open deck. The voyage encountered severe weather in the Atlantic and arrival at Baltimore & Ohio Pier 4, Locust Point, Baltimore, was some six days late on 20th February. There, waiting to help with the unloading, was Mr Riddles and his team, who had gone ahead separately. Messrs Bishop, Carswell and Soden had travelled on the liner *Aquitania* and had arrived in New York on 3rd February. They were able to enjoy a few days sight-seeing before Riddles arrived on 9th February. He had travelled on the *Queen Mary* with Col K. R. N. Speir, the LMS traffic officer for the Continent, who was in charge of the tour.

The Baltimore & Ohio Railroad was to be the principal host of the train. It had performed the same function for the Great Western's *King George V* in 1927. The company's president, Daniel Willard, who was seventy-eight years old, went to the docks to inspect the train on arrival. It was unloaded late in February and taken to the B&O's workshops at Mount Clare nearby to be put into running order. At the official ceremony of welcome in Baltimore on 17th March, Great Britain was represented by Captain Anthony Eden, the former foreign secretary who was then out of office. The train crew wore 'natty' business suits for the occasion with watch chains and bowler hats and the *B&O Magazine* reported: 'The Scot's engine crew ... are grand fellows. Everbody liked them and wanted to entertain them in Baltimore.'

Winter in the north east of the USA can be severe and the winter of 1939-40 was particularly bad. Unfortunately, Fred Bishop caught a heavy cold which turned into pneumonia and he had to enter a hospital in Baltimore. He thus missed the first public run on 18th March and so Carswell took charge of the engine, Riddles fired and W. C. Duvall, a veteran B&O engineman, gave a hand on the footplate and often took the regulator. His help in calling out the signal aspects was invaluable since Carswell did not at first realise that white was used to indicate clear. As well as conventional colour light signals, the B&O also used position lights at many places. These used seven white lights in a circular matrix to show horizontal, diagonal and vertical lines corresponding to a three-position semaphore signal.

The train went out to Point of Rocks, Maryland, with 250 newsmen and guests, and returned to Baltimore via Washington, where it stopped in the Union Station. Pictures were taken there alongside a B&O 'Royal Blue' Pacific, *President Lincoln*, a B&O diesel and a Pennsylvania Railroad class 'GG1' electric locomotive. A photo run followed with 'The Capitol Limited' hauled by the streamlined 'Royal Blue' engine and 'The Coronation Scot'. At the Thomas Viaduct over the Patusco River, originally built in 1835, the two trains were photographed both at rest and from a flat wagon

Plate 101: *Before departure the American tour train was displayed at Euston and a farewell ceremony took place on 9th January 1939. This view shows the personnel accompanying the train grouped round the cab of the engine. On the footplate are Driver F. C. Bishop and Fireman J. McKinnon Carswell; on the platform are F. A. Soden, a foreman in the erecting shops at Crewe, Master Mechanic, R. A. Riddles, then Mechanical and Electrical Engineer, Scotland, and Col K. R. N. Speir, Overseas and Continental Assistant to the Chief Commercial Manager.*

Plate 102: *No. 6220* Coronation, *formerly No. 6229, at Euston before departure to America. The headlamp required on railways in the United States is already in position, as is the buckeye coupler, and for the benefit of the press the bell is being lowered on to the engine as if in the process of being fitted; after the photographs had been taken it was removed again, as it was too high for the British loading gauge. On the platform watching operations are Driver Bishop and Fireman Carswell.*

Plate 103: *After being on display at Euston, the American train made a test run. It is seen here heading north near Wembley.*
Courtesy Dr Adrian H. Collyns

Plate 104: *Another view of the test train heading north accompanied by an aircraft, which is presumably carrying photographers; the location is between Berkhamstead and Tring.*
Courtesy Dr Adrian H. Collyns

Plate 105: Coronation *being loaded on board the* Belpamela *at Southampton. Driver Bishop and Fireman Carswell are watching proceedings from the quayside centre left.*
Courtesy Dr Adrian H. Collyns

Plate 106: *The Club Car being lowered into the hold.*
Courtesy Dr Adrian H. Collyns

Plate 107 (above): *An American stevedore helps to prepare* Coronation *for unloading after arrival in port at Baltimore. His dress is a good indication of the weather conditions at the time.*
Courtesy Adrian H. Collyns

Plate 108 (top right): Coronation *being lifted ashore from the* Belpamela *at Baltimore.* Courtesy Adrian H. Collyns

Plate 109 (right): *Driver Bishop and Fireman Mackinnon Carswell pose for the American press alongside* Coronation *before it is unloaded from the* Belpamela *at Baltimore.*
Courtesy Dr Adrian H. Collyns

Plate 110 (below): Coronation *backing its train out of Hartford, Connecticut station on the New York, New Haven & Hartford Rail Road.* Courtesy Dr Adrian H. Collyns

hauled ahead of them as they crossed the viaduct side by side. Another photo stop was made at St Denis where again the two trains ran side by side. On return to Washington an official luncheon was held and then another photo run took place out to Point of Rocks on the Potomac River, this time with 'The Capitol Limited' diesel-hauled.

Three days later, on Tuesday 21st March, 'The Coronation Scot' set off on its fast-moving three-and-a-half week tour. Its departure from Baltimore station was signalled remotely from the World's Fair in New York at exactly 10pm. The Baltimore & Ohio had planned the itinerary with great care so as to ensure a successful tour and probably never before or since has a single train been greeted with so much warmth and enthusiasm. At the larger towns and cities such as Chicago and Boston the train stopped for a whole day but at the smaller places the stops lasted only a matter of hours. Only a one-hour stop, for example, was scheduled at Kent, the hometown of Charles C. Green, the Director of Promotion of the World Fair; he was travelling with the train and using the first-class dining car as an exhibitions coach. At every stop, long or short, large crowds turned out to see the train and give it a warm welcome, and usually the local mayor was invited by Mr Riddles to open the exhibition. In all a total of thirty-seven mayors and eighteen governors was invited to visit the train and to accompany it as 'good-will ambassadors' for the fair, and no doubt many of them rode on it for various short sections. At Chicago the crew was given an American engine whistle by a local model railroad group. The B&O had already given the engine the bell mounted in front of the chimney.

The train's itinerary took it from Baltimore to Washington, Wilmington, Philadelphia, Lancaster, Harrisburg, Pittsburgh, Wheeling, Columbus, Dayton, Cincinnati, Louisville, Indianapolis, Terre Haute, St Louis, Springfield, Chicago, Kalamazoo, Battle Creek, Detroit, Toledo, Cleveland, Akron, Youngstown, Erie, Buffalo, Rochester, Syracuse, Utica, Schenectady, Albany, Springfield, Worcester, Boston, Providence, Hartford, New Haven and finally New York. Details of the dates it stopped at each place and the railways over which it worked are as follows:

Date	Railroad	Location
22nd March	Baltimore & Ohio	Washington, DC
23rd March	Pennsylvania	Wilmington, Del
23rd March	Pennsylvania	Philadelphia, Pa
24th March	Pennsylvania	Lancaster, Pa
24th March	Pennsylvania	Harrisburg, Pa
25th March	Pennsylvania	Pittsburg, Pa
26th March	Baltimore & Ohio	Wheeling, W Va
26-7th March	Baltimore & Ohio	Columbus, Ohio
27th March	Big Four	Dayton, Ohio
28th March	Big Four	Cincinatti, Ohio
29th March	Louisville & Nashville	Louisville, Ky
30th March	Louisville & Nashville	Indianapolis, Ind
30th March	Pennsylvania	Terre Haute, Ind
31st March	Pennsylvania	St Louis, Mo
1st April	Alton	Springfield, Ill
2nd April	Alton	Chicago, Ill
3rd April	Michigan Central	Kalamazoo, Mich
3rd April	Michigan Central	Battle Creek, Mich
4th April	Michigan Central	Detroit, Mich
5th April	New York Central	Toledo, Ohio
5-6th April	New York Central	Cleveland, Ohio
6th April	Baltimore & Ohio	Akron, Ohio
6th April	Baltimore & Ohio	Kent, Ohio
7th April	Baltimore & Ohio	Youngstown, Ohio
7th April	New York Central	Erie, Pa
8th April	New York Central	Buffalo, N Y
9th April	New York Central	Rochester, N Y
9th April	New York Central	Syracuse, N Y
10th April	New York Central	Utica, N Y
10th April	New York Central	Schenectady, N Y
11th April	New York Central	Albany, N Y
11th April	Boston & Albany	Springfield, Mass
12th April	Boston & Albany	Worcester, Mass
12-13th April	Boston & Albany	Boston, Mass
13th April	New York, New Haven & Hartford	Providence, R I
14th April	New York, New Haven & Hartford	Hartford, Conn
14th April	New York, New Haven & Hartford	New Haven, Conn

The train reached the Fairground in New York at 11pm on 14th April and went on display at the World's Fair. This was a vast exhibition, at which the railway section alone was large enough to constitute an exhibition in itself, covering an area of seventeen acres. It consisted of four main parts. 'Railroads in Building' was a cyclorama demonstrating the construction of railways and of their equipment. 'Railroads on Parade' was a presentation of the history of transport in America and had an amphitheatre seating 4000 people. Its outdoor stage was 250ft wide and 100ft deep; in addition to two standard-gauge tracks for the parade of engines and trains, both old and new, it accommodated broad highways, a performing stage for a cast of 250, and a channel in the background for the review of full-size replicas of historical ships. 'Railroads at Work' was a working model demonstrating the operation of a modern railway system. It was housed in a separate auditorium seating 1000 people and consisted of a scenic diorama 160ft wide and 40ft deep with 500 pieces of rolling stock.

The fourth part was a display of the latest American and foreign locomotives and trains, along with an old-time station yard housing other historic locomotives and rolling stock not featured in 'Railroads on Parade'. Among the latter were such historic engines as *Stourbridge Lion* of 1829, *John Bull*, which was sent to America in 1831 and was the first locomotive to run there, and New York Central 4-4-0 No. 999, which was reputed to have reached a speed of 112mph in 1893. One of the most impressive of the modern exhibits was a huge 6-4-4-6 streamlined express passenger engine which was mounted on rollers and ran at speed continuously; it was called *American Railways* and was built by the Pennsylvania Railroad.

The outstanding British exhibit in this section was of course 'The Coronation Scot', which stood alongside an Italian electric train in company with exhibits from Canada, the Soviet Union, France, Switzerland and Poland, as well as many more from America. It was calculated that more than two million people visited the train in 1939, including those who saw it during its tour. The one millionth visitor was recorded on 10th July at the World's Fair. She was Marguerite Temple, a young New York actress, who was greeted by Sir Louis Beale, the British Commissioner General to the fair,

Plate 111: Coronation *on display to the public at Hartford, Connecticut, with the Stars and Stripes and the Union Jack flanking the nameplate. The notice on the left reads:* THE CORONATION SCOT BRITAIN'S FAMOUS STREAMLINE TRAIN ON EXHIBITION.
Courtesy Kidderminster Railway Museum

Plate 112: *'The Coronation Scot' leaving Boston.* Courtesy Kidderminster Railway Museum

and later met Grover A. Whalen, the fair's president.

The year 1939, of course, was overshadowed by events in Europe, which culminated in the outbreak of the Second World War in September. At first the United States was not involved and the World's Fair closed for the winter as planned at the end of October. The men accompanying 'The Coronation Scot' returned to Great Britain and on 3rd November the train itself left New York for Baltimore where it was to be stored by the B&O for the winter. It was then for the LMS to decide whether to risk shipping it back across the Atlantic.

No decision was taken immediately, however, since the management of the World's Fair resolved to reopen it the following year despite the war. Accordingly in May 'The Coronation Scot' was restored to pristine condition in the carriage shops of the Long Island Rail Road and returned to the fair, where early visitors had already been enquiring as to its whereabouts. It was the month of Dunkirk and the large publicity folders presented to visitors now contained, in addition to pictures of peacetime travel in Great Britain, scenes of British railways at war. Lord Stamp was shown bidding farewell to Bishop and Carswell at Euston in 1939 and a new photograph now showed the trio in a similar pose but with all three men wearing steel helmets. 'In one period of eight days, the British railways conveyed over 300,000 troops in 620 special trains, whilst ... moving twenty million other passengers and six million tons of freight,' the folders said. A message over Lord Stamp's signature concluded by saying that the train in America was presented 'as an ambassador of British railways and as an example of British craftsmanship and technical achievement - qualities now bent to sterner duties. We present it also as a reminder of those ties and contacts - inevitably interrupted, if far from severed, by the differentiation between neutral and belligerent - which have so long bound us in mutual interest, and to whose restoration in full measure we confidently look forward when the war is over.'

When the fair finally closed *Coronation* was put into store at first but in 1941 it was decided that in view of the shortage of motive power it was worth the risk to ship it back and it arrived at Cardiff Docks on 16th February 1942. It was decided not to return 'The Coronation Scot' carriages during the war, however, and they were sent to the US Army's Quartermaster Corps Depot at Jeffersonville, Indiana, where they served as accommodation for officers. They remained in America until 1946. Sadly the man who was the driving force behind the visit of 'The Coronation Scot' to the United States did not himself survive the war. Lord Stamp, his wife and son were killed in an air raid on London in April 1941.

Plate 113: *The 'Coronation Scot' rounding Englishman's Curve on the Boston & Albany Rail Road in heavy rain. The location is at East Chatham, New York, and was so called because the photograph was taken by an English-born photographer who was an engineman on the B&A.*

Courtesy 'Railroading'

Chapter Four

POSTSCRIPT

As soon as war was declared on 3rd September 1939, the 'Coronation Scot' service was withdrawn. The last trains ran on 4th September and the coaches were put into store, two sets at Horwich and one at Lostock Hall. It was clearly the intention then for the service to be resumed when the war ended, and for some time new Pacifics still continued to be turned out of Crewe Works streamlined and in the red and gold livery. A batch of twenty was ordered in 1939, Nos 6235-54; they all had double chimneys, after the successful trials with No. 6234 *Duchess of Abercorn*, and the first ten were completed by July 1940. At least one of the original blue and silver engines, No. 6221 *Queen Elizabeth*, also appeared in red and gold being repainted after overhaul at Crewe early in 1941.

When the second ten of the order for twenty began to appear in June 1943, however, they were finished in plain unlined black with yellow numerals shaded in red. The first of these was No. 6245 *City of London*. From then on when earlier engines required repainting after overhaul they too were finished in plain wartime black.

As the war continued, it became increasingly obvious that streamlining itself was more of a hindrance than a help in wartime conditions. For almost any kind of repair, except for a few jobs such as work on fittings in the cab, the casing had to be taken off and put back in position when the work was completed. Skilled men of all kinds were in great demand during the war and any job which required more labour than was absolutely essential was clearly to be avoided. After fourteen of the 1939 order for twenty engines had been built streamlined, the remainder were built non-streamlined. They were closely similar to the prewar batch, Nos 6230-4, but had double chimneys from new and were painted plain black. The first of these was No. 6249 *City of Sheffield*.

The streamliners were magnificent machines and presented an inspiring spectacle sweeping along the main line whether in shiny prewar colours or in plain black. Indeed a grimy black steamliner at the head of one of the huge trains which were commonplace in the 1940s

Plate 114: *Resplendent in red and gold, No. 46235* City of Birmingham *takes water from Dillicar troughs with the 10am Glasgow-Euston on 24th August 1939. The double chimneys, of course, had a different profile, which enables these engines to be easily distinguished in photographs.* LCGB Ken Nunn Collection

Plate 115: *After the first ten streamlined Pacifics, five non-streamlined engines were built. They were followed by more streamlined engines, which had double chimneys, as a result of the successful trials with No. 6234* Duchess of Abercorn. *Like the second batch, they were painted in the red and gold livery and except for No. 6244* King George VI *they were all named after 'cities'. Here, No. 6236* City of Bradford *is seen on Crewe North shed with unstreamlined No. 6233* Duchess of Sutherland *in the summer of 1939.*
W. H. Whitworth

Plate 116: *The red and gold livery was applied to the third batch of streamliners, Nos. 6235-44, even though the last six appeared after the start of the Second World War. Here, on 27th June 1940, two fitters secure the nameplate* King George VI *to the casing of No. 6244, for the benefit of a press photographer . The spring-loaded fasteners on the access hatches can be clearly seen.*
Courtesy Adrian H. Collyns

Plate 117: *In a scene familiar to many who stood on the footbridge across the north end of Crewe station in the days of steam, the last 'Coronation' to be streamlined, No. 46243* City of Lancaster, *arrives with an up express in 1948. The load is probably fifteen or sixteen coaches but the back of the train is hidden by smoke drifting across from Crewe North shed.*
Leonard Hobdey, courtesy Michael Bentley

Plate 118: *No. 6239* City of Chester, *its red and gold livery now replaced by plain black, stands outside the paint shop at Crewe Works on 5th May 1946, after intermediate repairs. Alongside is 0-4-2 Bissel tank No. 7865.*

Harry Townley, courtesy Michael Bentley

Plate 119: *A shed labourer cleans ashes out of the smokebox of a grimy streamliner on 14th March 1944. Normally, enginemen were required to check that the smokebox door was tightly fastened as part of their routine 'preparation' of an engine before a run; but it seems that the streamliners were an exception to this rule and that the responsibility rested with the shed staff who had disposed of the engine earlier. Presumably this was to avoid the necessity of having to re-open the doors in the casing. Certainly a Crewe North fireman who regularly worked on the streamliners does not recall ever checking the smokebox before a run.* Courtesy Dr Adrian H. Collyns

was just as imposing in its way as was its blue or red counterpart in the immaculate state of the late 1930s. The plain black paint served to emphasise the size and power of the machine. Some writers, who probably never saw one, have described the streamliners, especially the black ones, as 'bulbous ugly monsters'. At best, this is an opinion, but it is one considered by many observers as 'rubbish'. A grimy black streamliner emerging from the mist on a freezing cold day in the winter of 1946-7 at the head of 16 coaches was an awe-inspring sight, never to be forgotten.

Despite their impressive appearance, however, their demise was not altogether a matter for regret on the part of the enginemen who worked on them. A former fireman at Crewe North, who worked on the streamliners regularly, and whose views are probably typical, feels that they were unequalled in their performance by any other main-line express engine in Great Britain. As well as their high-speed exploits, they were masters of Shap and Beattock and even if stopped at Scout Green with 540 tons could restart the train without difficulty. Yet they had certain features that often gave rise to the feeling that 'the man who designed these b..... things ought to have to work on them'!

This was because they were more difficult to service and prepare at the sheds, and to work on generally than the non-streamlined engines. Because the cab was more enclosed, it was hotter, and so putting on a fire under the low roof at Camden shed was rather like having a Turkish bath. Then again, to fill the sandboxes it was necessary first to walk round the shed to find a suitable ladder, one which would hook over the handrails. When one had been found and put in position, the fireman had to climb up with a bucket full of sand, remove the filler cap and pour the sand into the opening, an operation requiring skill, care and strength. Because of the size of the opening of the pipe, a lot of sand would be spilt unless the fireman was extremely careful. In fact, the streamliners were not the only Stanier engines whose sandboxes were far from easy to fill. They generally had filler pipes which were tucked under the curve of the boiler so that it was impossible to hold a bucket vertically above the pipe opening and pour sand directly into it. Inevitably a lot

Plate 120: *No. 6229* Duchess of Hamilton *on the up slow line just south of Basford Hall in August 1944. The engine is probably still in the red and gold paint in which it went to America, as the stripes and 'LMS' are just visible on the tender, but it is so dirty that its identity is only known from the photographer's notes.* Harry Townley, courtesy Michael Bentley

of sand was spilt on the footplating, and the fireman often ended up pushing and flicking it into the pipe. A better design of sand-bucket would have helped to solve the problem.

Ladders were also needed to enable the fireman to fill the oilboxes and attend to the lubricators on the frames. Access to these was by means of a hinged flap with two spring-loaded catches; occasionally the catches would jam and need to be 'persuaded' with the large $^{7}/_{8}$in spanner.

Another factor was that the streamlined casing enclosing the boiler, cylinders and front end tended to keep the heat inside and keep out the air flow which cooled a conventional engine. This meant that it was very hot underneath when oiling round and preparing for a run, and the job was made still more difficult because it was always dark under the casing and so lamps were needed underneath, even in daylight, especially when the engine was in the shed.

There is no evidence incidentally that because the streamlined engines ran hotter they were troubled by hot big ends. Theoretically they would have used more oil; but the amount of oil used was always considerable anyway on both streamlined and non-streamlined engines, and great attention had to be paid to oiling in both cases, as the engines worked long distances. If there was any difference in the amount of oil used, it was of no importance so far as the authorities were concerned.

The streamlined tenders also caused problems. Firstly, they were always relatively dirty to work on. Despite the fitting of a cover with a lip on its rear edge over the front of the tender, as a result of the wind tunnel tests, the problem of coal dust being sucked into the cab as the coal was used was never completely solved. The effect was particularly noticeable when running under easy steam with no side winds. The exhaust would then drift along the top of the boiler and be sucked into the tender, where the coal had been removed, and draw smoke and steam into the cab. Even if it did not draw coal dust in with it, it still created unpleasant working conditions.

In the event, however, this was not the immediate reason for the removal of the covers. Because they restricted the amount of coal that could be loaded on the front of the tender, instructions were issued for their removal in June 1943, so as to increase coal capacity in preparation for the resumption of through workings to Scotland in the following October.

Another problem with the streamlined tenders resulted from the rearward extension of the side sheeting. Two tank fillers were provided, one on each side, and sliding panels in the sheeting gave access to them. The engine had to be stopped precisely opposite the water column and the leather 'bag' had to be manoeuvred through the door. This was not easy even in normal conditions. On the former LNWR section, for example, the water columns had wide leather bags which would only just go through the sliding panels in the tender sides. The fireman often had to do a lot of 'twisting and pulling about' to get the bag through and sometimes, if the bag was twisted, it might cause an air lock.

All this became much more difficult in severe winter weather when the bag was frozen stiff with ice. Typical of the kind of problems that could be encountered then was a run on an overnight Scotch train when the streamliner working through from Glasgow was remanned at Crewe. It was a very cold night, with snow

Plate 121: *No. 46243* City of Lancaster *with the 10am Glasgow-Euston on 24th May 1947 south of Tring. Thanks to the absence of exhaust, the outline of the double chimney is clearly seen.* LCGB Ken Nunn collection

Plate 122: *No. 6244* King George VI *passing Kenton with the 10am from Euston to Glasgow on 26th May 1947. The tender is typical of the period: it has lost its shrouding over the coal space and the rearward streamlined extension but it retains the shrouding over the springs. Loads of fifteen or sixteen coaches as here were common at this time.* LCGB Ken Nunn collection

and hard frost. For some reason, perhaps because of the freezing weather, very little water was picked up at Hademore troughs and so it was decided to stop at Nuneaton to fill the tank. There the bag had frozen solid, in spite of the usual coal fire in the brazier; when the water was turned on, it helped to loosen the bag slightly, but the combined efforts of the driver and fireman, as well as the vigorous use of the coal hammer, were needed to manhandle the bag through the restricted gap in the top of the tender. The delay caused in this way was about 25 minutes.

Thus in July 1945 it was decided to cut away the rear panels on the streamlined tenders to the same shape as those of the non-streamlined engines, so as to facilitate the filling of the tank. The shrouding over the springs was not removed at this time and the tenders modified in this way ran in a hybrid form for a while. Even later, when this shrouding had been removed, the tenders which had been built streamlined were still recognisable by the shape of the side panels at the front above

Plate 123: *No. 6236* City of Bradford *passing Eglinton Street station on the 5.40pm Glasgow-Euston in July 1947.*
C. L. Kerr, courtesy Kidderminster Railway Museum

Plate 124: *No. 6226* Duchess of Norfolk *in Crewe Works after overhaul in September 1946. It lost its steamlinging less than a year later.*
W. Potter, courtesy Kidderminster Railway Museum

Plate 125: *No. 6239* City of Chester, *its black paint somewhat grimy, passes Willesden Junction with the 8.30pm from Euston to Liverpool on 9th May 1947. The back of the train disappears into the mist but the load was normally fifteen or sixteen coaches at that time.*
LCGB Ken Nunn collection

Plate 126: *No. 6243* City of Lancaster *near Tring with the 1.15pm from Euston to Glasgow on 5th September 1947. Its condition is typical of the war and postwar era, though even then it was exceptional for the cover giving access to the lubricators to be left undone as here.*
LCGB Ken Nunn collection

Plate 127: *All the streamliners were destreamlined in 1946-7 except for* City of Lancaster, *which was converted only in May 1949. It thus became the only streamliner to receive a British Railways number and is seen here as 46243 on Crewe North shed.*
W. H. Whitworth

Plate 128: *No. 46243* City of Lancaster *at Crewe on 7th May 1949, only days before the streamlining was removed. It is probably standing on Crewe South shed, waiting to be taken into the works.*
A. G. Ellis collection

the handrail, where they retained the original higher profile compared with that of tenders which were built non-streamlined.

None of the problems with the streamliners were anything but minor, nor did they detract from the performance of the engines on the road, which was superb. But the reasons which justified streamlining in time of peace, its publicity value and economy in high-speed running, no longer applied. Throughout the war and in the immediate postwar period huge trains were run, packed to capacity, and journey times were greatly extended. There was no place for high-speed trains of eight or nine coaches.

When the war ended, the economic climate in the country was such that there was no possibility of an immediate reintroduction of 'The Coronation Scot' or any other lightweight high-speed service. The labour situation was still very difficult and so eventually the company decided to abandon streamlining altogether, the instruction for its removal being issued in December 1945. The first engine to be converted was No. 6235 *City of Birmingham*, which first appeared from Crewe Works without its streamlined casing in April 1946, and the last No. 46243 *City of Lancaster* in May 1949; by surviving in streamlined form so long, the latter became the only streamlined Pacific to carry its BR number. The smokeboxes of the streamlined engines had sloped downwards at the top to suit the shape of the casing at the front end and at first the converted engines retained this distinctive slope. In time, howev-

Plate 129: *When the 'Coronation Scot' service was suspended at the outbreak of war, the carriages were repainted in normal colours and put into ordinary service. Here, restaurant third open No. 8993, now with 'M' prefix and suffix, is seen in the early BR red and cream livery at Derby on 30th April 1956.*
H. C. Casserley, courtesy Richard M. Casserley

er, they received smokeboxes of the usual circular shape and so became virtually indistinguishable from the original non-streamlined engines.

The Carriages
Except for the sleeping car and club car, the train which went to America was part of one of the train sets which it was intended to introduce on 'The Coronation Scot' service in 1940. The onset of the Second World War prevented a complete train from being built at that time but the outstanding vehicles were eventually completed after the war with the exception of the kitchen cars. The articulated twin kitchen car and open third which went to America, therefore, remained a unique set.

As well as nine articulated twin sets, the postwar vehicles included five single carriages, of which three were corridor thirds and two open thirds. The latter seem likely to have been intended to run with two single kitchen cars and so perhaps it was considered undesirable to have a kitchen car as part of a twin set - it has been suggested that the set which went to America did not ride well. Whatever the reason, the two postwar 'Coronation Scot' sets could have been made up of nine, ten or eleven coaches, by the omission or inclusion of the single carriages. The American set with its postwar additions could have been made up to consist of either ten or eleven carriages. In this way the accommodation provided by these sets could have been adjusted, to some extent at any rate, to suit traffic levels. They would thus have had a degree of flexibility that is often lacking in set trains. The club saloon which went to America seems not to have been intended to have a regular place in the 'Coronation Scot' sets but doubtless it could have been added on occasion if required for special parties. Clearly it performed a useful function on the American tour but what role, if any, it was intended for on return to Great Britain is uncertain.

The three 1940 sets would have been made up as follows:

Set	BFK+FK*	FK+RFO*	RK+RTO*		RTO+TK	TK	BTK+TK
1	56010-1	56100-1	56200-1		56300-1	2148	56500-1
	BFK+FK	FK+RFO	RK	TO	RTO+TK	TK	BTK+TK
2	56002-3	56102-3		9517	56302-3	2149	56502-3
	BFK+FK	FK+RFO	RK	TO	RTO+TK	TK	BTK+TK
3	56004-5	56104-5		9518	56304-5	2150	56504-5

* vehicles which went to America.

Plate 130: *Another restaurant third open, No. M9004M, at Llanfairfechan on 26th August 1964. The higher viewpoint shows more detail of the carriage roof and the streamlined housing of the ventilation system.*
H. C. Casserley, courtesy Richard M. Casserley

Plate 131: *When the 'Coronation Scot' stock returned from America in 1946, it was repainted in normal LMS colours and put into ordinary service. Here articulated twin BFK/FK Nos. M56000/1M are seen in BR maroon livery at Colwyn Bay on 3rd August 1963. They were withdrawn in January 1965.*
Richard M. Casserley

Plate 132: *'Coronation Scot' stock of the type which went to America, ordered before the war was not completed by the LMS and BR until the early 1950s. Here corridor third No. M2149M, one of three built in 1947-9, stands at Stamford on 11th April 1963.* Richard M. Casserley

Plate 133: *Articulated twin RTO/TK Nos. M56304/5M, built in May 1948, at Verney Junction on 15th February 1957.* Richard M. Casserley

Plate 134: *Club saloon No. M823M, one of the vehicles which went to America, in the 'Cambrian Radio Cruise Train' at Aberdovey on 19th July 1956. It is painted in the early BR livery of red and cream.* F. W. Shuttleworth

Despite the construction of these vehicles, no attempt was made to reintroduce 'The Coronation Scot' after the Second World War. The three original sets of coaches, which spent the war in storage, never ran as set trains again. Their coaches were repainted in standard LMS colours and were put into ordinary service in 1947. When the American stock returned to Great Britain in 1946 it too was repainted in standard LMS colours and again mostly put into normal service. The exceptions were the club car and the articulated twin kitchen car and third open. At first these were stored for a while at Craven Arms. Then in May 1948 the twin set was moved to Derby where it remained in store for some time; it was the first articulated set to be withdrawn and broken up, which supports the suggestion that it rode badly. Quite probably, it never ran in service in Great Britain. The club car was eventually used in the 'North Wales Land Cruise' train in 1953-4 and subsequently on various special workings. All the new post-war vehicles were also turned out in the standard livery of the day and put into normal service.

Possibilities

If the new 'Coronation Scot' train sets had been put into service in 1940, they would, of course. have been hauled by streamlined 'Coronation' class Pacifics in red

Plate 135: *Another view of club saloon No. M823M on the same occasion as the previous picture. On the left is former Midland Railway semi-royal saloon No. 809.* F. W. Shuttleworth

Plate 136: *Club saloon No. M823M at Glasson Dock on 1st May 1954 during the 'North Lancashire Tour' organised jointly by the Stephenson Locomotive Society and the Manchester Locomotive Society.* F. W. Shuttleworth

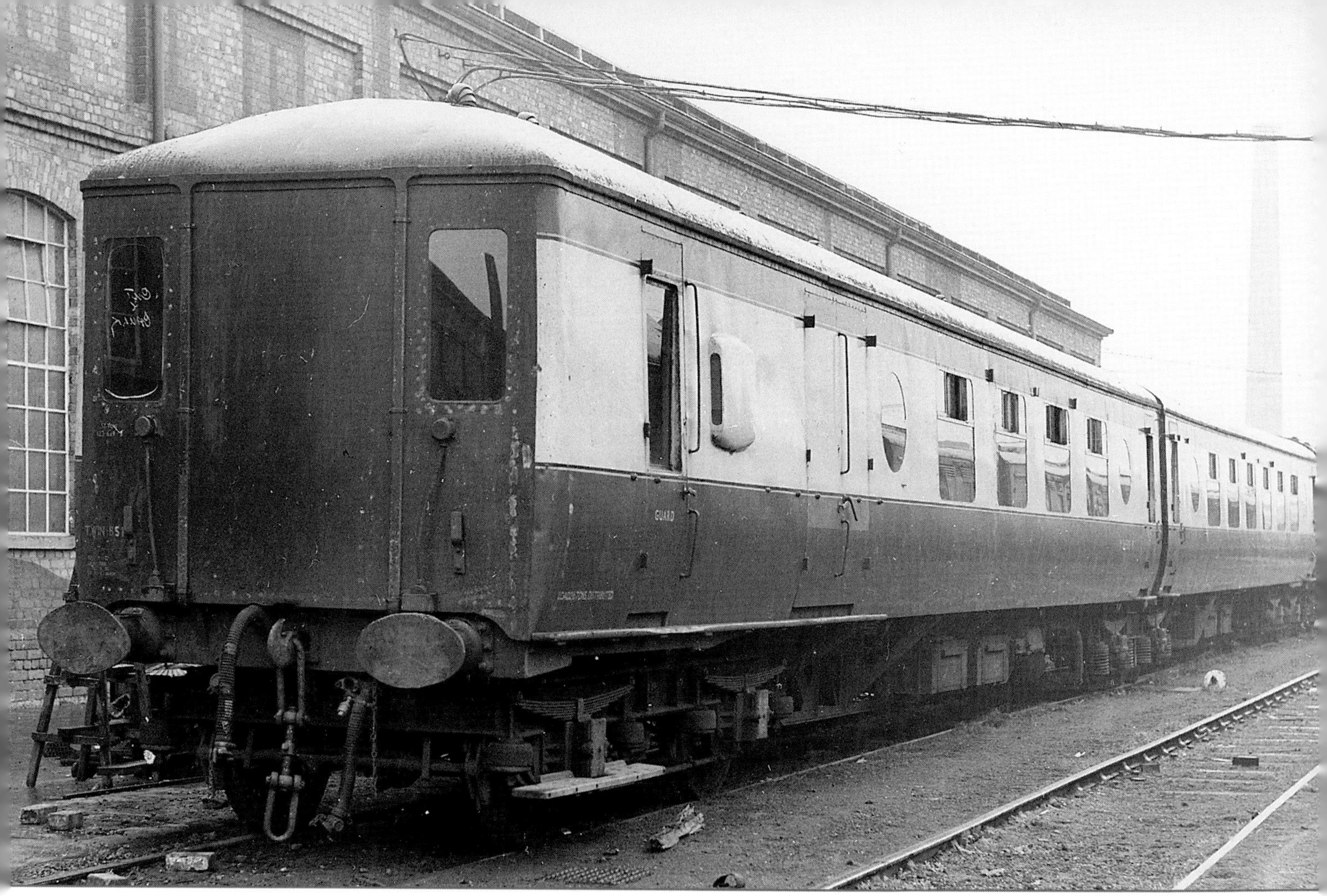

Plate 137: *BTK/TK Nos. M56502/3 at Wolverton Works on 2nd February 1958.* T. J. Edgington

and gold paint. Sadly such a development was not to be and in fact 'The Coronation Scot' never ran between Euston and Glasgow in that livery. Nevertheless, if the Second World War had not prevented its plans from coming to fruition, the LMS would have developed its high-speed services further. Schemes were already under consideration to do away with the small high-speed train of some nine coaches weighing 300 tons in favour of 500-ton expresses travelling at the same speed. Scheduling one train at higher speed than other expresses on the same line had harmful effects on line occupation. Trains in front of it had to be sidetracked and held while it passed and those behind it followed at increasingly greater intervals. These effects were undesirable and unacceptable on a main line as busy as the West Coast route to Scotland. The solution which the LMS authorities decided to aim for was to raise the overall speed of all expresses to that of 'The Coronation Scot' and so to establish a new norm.

To work 500-ton trains at 'Coronation Scot' speeds more powerful engines would have been required and outline schemes for such machines were in fact worked out. They would have been based on the 'Coronation' class but would have had the 4-6-4 wheel arrangement to allow a larger firebox, with a larger grate and ashpan, and a generally increased boiler capacity. Boiler pressure would have been 300lb psi, grate area 70 sq ft, cylinders $17^1/_2$in by 28in, instead of $16^1/_2$in by 28in, and 6ft 6in driving wheels. A mechanical stoker would have been essential - indeed it was beyond the ability of one man to fire a 'Coronation' at maximum output - and an eight-wheeled tender holding 12 tons of coal and 5000 gallons of water would have been fitted. As an interim step, two 'Super Pacifics' with re-designed high-capacity boilers of 300lb psi, were authorised in June 1939. Unfortunately, they were cancelled in January 1943 since there was no need for them in wartime conditions. So the potential of such a design will never be known.

On 1st January 1948 the LMS disappeared as a separate entity and became part of the nationalised British Railways. The difficulties of the early postwar era at first prevented the introduction of any light-weight high-speed service and when things improved it was 'The Caledonian' that was introduced with standard BR Mark I stock rather than any revived 'Coronation Scot'. Sadly the short time for which 'The Coronation Scot' ran, three summers and two winters, was thus only a brief indication of what the LMS might have achieved if the course of history and progress had been different.

APPENDIXES

Appendix One - 'Princess Coronation' Class Engine History Details

No.	*Name*	*Order No*	*Date*	*Cost engine/tender*	*Tender No*	*Double chimney fitted*	*Streamlining removed*	*Date of BR number*	*Smoke deflectors fitted*	*Sloping smokebox replaced*	*Withdrawn*
6220	*Coronation*	402	6.1937	£11813/1556	9703	12.1944	9.1946	7.1948	On removal	2.1957	4.1963
6221	*Queen Elizabeth*	402	6.1937	£11813/1556	9704	11.1940	5.1946	10.1948	of	9.1952	5.1963
6222	*Queen Mary*	402	6.1937	£11813/1556	9705	8.1943	5.1946	9.1948	streamlining	8.1953	10.1963
6223	*Princess Alice*	402	7.1937	£11813/1556	9706	11.1941	8.1946	3.1949	"	8.1955	10.1963
6224	*Princess Alexandra*	402	7.1937	£11813/1556	9707	5.1940	5.1946	5.1948	"	10.1954	10.1963
6225	*Duchess of Gloucester*	408	5.1938	£10136/1601	9743	6.1943	2.1947	6.1948	"	1.1955	9.1964
6226	*Duchess of Norfolk*	408	5.1938	£10136/1601	9744	7.1942	6.1947	9.1948	"	11.1955	9.1964
6227	*Duchess of Devonshire*	408	6.1938	£10136/1601	9745	12.1940	2.1947	5.1948	"	5.1953	12.1962
6228	*Duchess of Rutland*	408	6.1938	£10136/1601	9746	9.1940	7.1947	7.1948	"	1.1957	9.1964
6229	*Duchess of Hamilton*	408	9.1938	£10136/1601	9747	4.1943	11.1947	7.1948	"	2.1957	2.1964+
6230	*Duchess of Buccleuch*	408	6.1938	£9585/1509	9748	10.1940		5.1948	9.1946		11.1963
6231	*Duchess of Atholl*	408	6.1938	£9585/1509	9749	6.1940		5.1948	9.1946		12.1962
6232	*Duchess of Montrose*	408	7.1938	£9585/1509	9750	1.1943		5.1948	2.1945		12.1962
6233	*Duchess of Sutherland*	408	7.1938	£9585/1509	9751	3.1941		10.1948	9.1946		2.1964+
6234	*Duchess of Abercorn*	408	8.1938	£9585/1509	9752	2.1939		10.1948	3.1946		1.1963
6235	*City of Birmingham*	414	7.1939	£9437/1549	9798		4.1946	5.1948	On removal	7.1952	9.1964+
6236	*City of Bradford*	414	7.1939	£9437/1549	9799		12.1947	4.1948	of	11.1953	3.1964
6237	*City of Bristol*	414	8.1939	£9437/1549	9800		1.1947	7.1948	streamlining	5.1956	9.1964
6238	*City of Carlisle*	414	9.1939	£9437/1549	9801		11.1946	3.1949	"	10.1953	9.1964
6239	*City of Chester*	414	9.1939	£9437/1549	9802		6.1947	8.1948	"	2.1957	9.1964
6240	*City of Coventry*	414	3.1940	£9437/1549	9803		6.1947	6.1948	"	5.1957	9.1964
6241	*City of Edinburgh*	414	4.1940	£9437/1549	9804		1.1947	5.1948	"	2.1958	9.1964
6242	*City of Glasgow*	414	5.1940	£9437/1549	9805		3.1947	5.1948	"	11.1953	10.1963
6243	*City of Lancaster*	414	6.1940	£9437/1549	9806		5.1949	4.1948	"	11.1958	9.1964
6244	*King George VI*	414	7.1940	£9437/1549	9807		8.1947	8.1948	"	7.1953	9.1964
6245	*City of London*	415	6.1943	£9324/1670	9808		8.1947	8.1948	"	12.1957	9.1964
6246	*City of Manchester*	415	8.1943	£10182/1670	9809		9.1946	11.1948	"	5.1960	1.1963
6247	*City of Liverpool*	415	9.1943	£9037/1670	9810		5.1947	11.1948	"	5.1958	5.1963
6248	*City of Leeds*	415	10.1943	£9445/1670	9811		12.1946	3.1949	"	6.1958	9.1964
6249	*City of Sheffield*	415	4.1944	£10069/1670	9812			4.1948	11.1946		11.1963
6250	*City of Lichfield*	415	5.1944	£10069/1670	9813			2.1949	3.1946		9.1964
6251	*City of Nottingham*	415	6.1944	£10069/1670	9814			5.1948	8.1946		9.1964
6252	*City of Leicester*	415	6.1944	£10069/1670	9815			4.1949	3.1945		5.1963
6253	*City of St. Albans*	464	9.1946	£15460/	9816			9.1949			1.1963
6254	*City of Stoke-on-Trent*	464	9.1946	£15460/	9817			7.1949			9.1964
6255	*City of Hereford*	464	10.1946	£15460/	10622			6.1949			9.1964
6256	*Sir William A. Stanier F. R. S.*	464	12.1947	£18248/3163	10623			5.1948			10.1964
6257	*City of Salford*	464	2.1948	£18248/3163	10624			5.1948			9.1964

* *City of Leeds* until 4.1941
\+ preserved.
Order numbers were the same for engines and tenders but prefixed 'E' and 'T' accordingly.
'Cost' is completed cost averaged over each batch.

Summary of condition when new

Although there were only thirty-eight engines in the class, they differed widely in their external appearance when new. The following table summarises the main features of difference:

6220-6224	Streamlined, blue, single chimney
6225-6229	Streamlined, red, single chimney
6230-6234	Not streamlined, red, single chimney, no smoke deflectors
6235-6244	Streamlined, red, double chimney
6245-6248	Streamlined, black, double chimney
6249-6252	Not streamlined, black, double chimney, no smoke deflectors, streamlined tenders
6253-6256	Not streamlined, black 1946 livery, double chimney, smoke deflectors
6257	Not streamlined, black 1946 livery, double chimney, smoke deflectors, completed as 6257M but changed to 46257 with 'BRITISH RAILWAYS' on tender before entering service.

Appendix Two

Instructions to Signalmen for the Working of the 'Coronation Scot'

E.R.O. 46436/2229.
OP. 2.

LONDON MIDLAND AND SCOTTISH RAILWAY COMPANY.

OK. Crewe/South.

Instructions to Signalmen for the Working of the Coronation Scot Train Euston to Glasgow and Glasgow to Euston.

The Regulations for Train Signalling on Double lines by the Absolute Block System, or Permissive (Station Yard) Block System where such is in operation, apply with the following modifications and additions.

BLOCK REGULATIONS.

Regulation 3.

These trains must be signalled by the special "Is line clear" signal 4–4–4.

Where necessary in order to avoid delay the special "Is line clear" signal 4–4–4 must, provided the "Train out of section" signal has been received for the previous train and the block indicator is in the normal position, be sent forward as soon as the special "Is line clear" signal has been acknowledged to the signal box in rear and before the "Train entering section" signal is received, except at those places where the special "Is line clear" signal has to be acknowledged by the signal box in advance before it is acknowledged to the signal box in rear.

Regulation 4.

In clear weather, and during fog or falling snow when the fogsignalmen are on duty, the special "Is line clear" signal 4–4–4 must not be acknowledged to the signal box in rear unless :—

(1) All the necessary points worked or controlled from the signal box have been placed in their proper position for the safety of the train.

(2) The line upon which the train is timed to run is clear for ¼ mile beyond the home or outermost home signal and if there is a stop signal or signals ahead of this point (including intermediate block signals) the line is clear to the last stop signal,

OR

The line is clear for ¼ mile beyond the home or outermost home signal and the preceding train, with tail lamp attached, is continuing on its journey and all the signals (including intermediate block signals) have been taken off for it to proceed into the section in advance.

Where special instructions for the signalling of through trains are in force they will apply to these trains.

At the following signal boxes on the lines shown, in clear weather, and during fog or falling snow when the fogsignalmen are on duty, the special "Is line clear" signal 4–4–4 must not be

Except as provided for in the preceding paragraph, where the signal box in advance is less than 880 yards ahead, in clear weather, and during fog or falling snow when the fogsignalmen are on duty, clause (b) of this regulation must be applied. This instruction will also apply at the following boxes :—

Down line—Queen's Park No. 1, Willesden No. 7, Sudbury Junction, Nash Mills, Bourne End, Tring Cutting, Sears Crossing, Stoke Hammond, Lamb's Siding, Bletchley No. 3, Denbigh Hall, Loughton Goods Sidings, Castlethorpe Station, Hanslope, Ashton, Welton Station, Kilsby Tunnel North End, Rugby No. 7, Shilton No. 1, Bulkington Station, Attleboro', Ashby Junction, Hartshill Sidings, Atherstone Station, Polesworth Station, Tamworth No. 2, Hademore Crossing, Lichfield (T.V.) No. 2, Colwich Station, Norton Bridge Junction, Standon Bridge Station, Wrine Hill, Basford Hall Junction, Crewe North Junction.

Up line — Crewe Coal Yard, Basford Sand Sidings, Betley Road Station, Wrine Hill, Madeley Station, Whitmore Station, Standon Bridge Station, Norton Bridge Junction, Milford & Brocton, Rugeley (T.V.) No. 1, Armitage Station, Lichfield (T.V.) No. 1, Hademore Crossing, Coton Crossing, Tamworth No. 1, Baddesley Sidings, Hartshill Sidings, Nuneaton No. 1, Clifton Road Junction, Hillmorton Sidings, Kilsby Tunnel South End, Blisworth Station, Roade Station, Ashton, Hanslope, Loughton Goods Sidings, Denbigh Hall, Bletchley No. 1, Lamb's Siding, Stoke Hammond, Sears Crossing, Cheddington Station, Tring Cutting, Bourne End, Nash Mills, Sudbury Junction, Brent Junction, Willesden No. 1, Queen's Park No. 2.

Should the block apparatus between two signal boxes less than 880 yards apart have failed, the special " Is line clear " signal 4-4-4 must not be acknowledged by repetition, but provided it has been ascertained that the line is clear as far as can be seen and all points necessary for the safety of the approaching train have been placed in their proper position, the special " Is line clear " signal 4-4-4 must be acknowledged in accordance with Regulation 5. The Signalman to whom this signal is sent must be advised previously of the circumstances.

Clause (e).

During fog or falling snow before the fogsignalmen are on duty, before permission is given for the train signalled by the special " Is line clear " signal 4-4-4 to approach, a detonator must be placed on the rail in every case unless the train has been accepted by the signal box in advance.

Regulation 33.

At a signal box controlling a level crossing the gates must be closed to the roadway, if not already in that position, immediately the special " Is line clear " signal 4-4-4 has been acknowledged to the signal box in rear.

OTHER INSTRUCTIONS.

Should it be necessary for the train to be diverted on to a line other than that on which it usually travels, the Signalman at the signal box in rear must be advised and instructed to bring the train to a stand and verbally inform the Driver of the circumstances, advising the Signalman at the signal box where the train is to be diverted that this has been done. On receipt of this information the special " Is line clear " signal 4-4-4 may be acknowledged in accordance with standard Regulation 4 or any modifications or additions to this Regulation included on the special instructions exhibited in the signal box.

WORKING OF INTERMEDIATE LEVEL CROSSINGS.

At level crossings where the gates are operated by a Crossing Keeper and where telephone or bell communication is provided between such crossing and the adjacent signal box or boxes, the Signalmen at the box or boxes concerned must, before acknowledging the special " Is line clear " signal 4-4-4, carry out the following instructions :—

Where bell communication is provided.

A special bell code 4-4-4 must be sent to and acknowledged by repetition by the Crossing Keeper. This code will be acknowledged when the crossing gates are across the roadway.

Where telephone communication is provided.

Ascertain that the gates are closed to the roadway and instruct the Crossing Keeper to keep them in this position until the train has passed over the crossing and the conditions are such that the Crossing Keeper is in a position to open the gates to the roadway in accordance with the normal method of working.

Euston Station,
July, 1937.

BY ORDER OF THE
CHIEF OPERATING MANAGER.

Appendix Three - Summary Details of 'Coronation Scot' Coaching Stock

Builders: Wol: LMS Wolverton Works; Derby: LMS Derby Works; Glo: Gloucester Railway Carriage & Wagon; BCW: Birmingham Railway Carriage & Wagon; MetCam: Metropolitan Cammell.
Withdrawal dates are by LMS four-weekly periods (thirteen to the year).
'Cost' is 'First Cost', a book-keeping figure, and for conversions is the same as the unconverted coaches.

The 1937 Stock

Diagram	*Type*	*Lot*	*No.*	*Built*	*Date*	*Cost*	*Wdn*
D1961	BFK	1063	5052	Wol	25.5.37	£2142	12.64
D1961	BFK	1063	5053	Wol	29.6.37	£2142	11.64
D1961	BFK	1063	5054	Wol	10.8.37	£2142	4.64
D1960	FK	1062	1069	Wol	25.5.37	£2395	12.64
D1960	FK	1062	1070	Wol	29.6.37	£2395	12.63
D1960	FK	1062	1071	Wol	10.8.37	£2395	11.64
D1902	RFO	734	7507	Wol	4.34	£2025	1.64
D1902	RFO	734	7508	Wol	4.34	£2025	12.63
D1902	RFO	734	7509	Wol	4.34	£2025	13.62
D1912	RK	956	30084	Glo	8.36	£2556	13.62
D1912	RK	956	30085	Glo	8.36	£2556	6.63
D1912	RK	956	30086	Glo	8.36	£2556	13.62
D1912	RK	956	30087	Glo	8.36	£2556	13.63
D1912	RK	956	30088	Glo	9.36	£2556	7.56
D1912	RK	956	30089	Glo	9.36	£2556	13.62
D1981	RTO	804	8931	MetCam	5.34	£2008	10.62
D1981	RTO	804	8950	MetCam	6.34	£2008	10.64
D1981	RTO	804	8961	MetCam	6.34	£2008	1.64
D1981	RTO	805	8993	BCW	6.34	£2008	11.63
D1981	RTO	805	8996	BCW	6.34	£2008	8.62
D1981	RTO	805	9003	BCW	7.34	£2008	9.62
D1981	RTO	805	9004	BCW	7.34	£2008	11.64
D1981	RTO	805	9006	BCW	7.34	£2008	13.63
D1981	RTO	805	9029	BCW	8.34	£2008	11.62
D1905	BTK	898	5729	Derby	8.36	£1406	9.64
D1905	BTK	898	5812	Derby	8.36	£1406	8.64
D1905	BTK	898	5814	Derby	9.36	£1406	12.64

Disposals/broken up (where known):
Kings of Norwich: 5054 5.64; 7507 2.65; 30084 4.64; 8931 8.63; 8950 11.64; 9003 12.63; 9029 11.63.
Taylor Bros, Trafford Park: 1070 12.63.
Birds, Long Marston: 6.64.
Sheppey (Ship-breaking Co, Queenborough): 7509 10.63.
Derby: 8993 11.63.
Central Wagon Co, Ince: 8996 8.62; 9004 11.64.
30084 was converted to CCE inspection saloon at Wolverton in 2.58 and is still in service.

The 1940 Stock

Diagram	*Type*	*Lot*	*No.*	*Built*	*Date*	*Cost*	*Wdn*
D2014	BFK/FK	1148	56000-1	Derby	.39	£5840x2	1.65
D2014	BFK/FK	1176A	56002-3	Derby	12.47	£4595x2	11.65
D2014	BFK/FK	1176A	56004-5	Derby	12.47	£4595x2	4.65
D2015	FK/RFO	1149	56100-1	Derby	.38	£6249/6250	2.64
D2138	FK/RFO	1177A	56102-3	Derby	1.48	£4583/4582	11.65
D2138	FK/RFO	1177A	56104-5	Derby	5.48	£4582x2	4.64
D2016	RK/RTO	1150	56200-1	Derby	.39	£6247/6248	4.52
D2017	RTO/TK	1151A	56300-1	Derby	12.47	£4902/4903	3.66
D2017	RTO/TK	1179A	56302-3	Derby	5.48	£4415/4414	11.65
D2017	RTO/TK	1179A	56304-5	Derby	5.48	£4415/4414	4.65
D2018	BTK/TK	1153A	56500-1	Derby	12.47	£4207/4206	12.66
D2018	BTK/TK	1181	56502-3	Derby	4.49	£3818/3817	6.64
D2018	BTK/TK	1181A	56504-5	Derby	5.51	£3818x2	13.63
D2020	Club	1164	823	Derby	.39	£4669	4.63
D2019	TK	1152A	2148	Derby	12.47	£4348	10.67
D2019	TK	1180A	2149	Derby	8.49	£4673	11.67
D2019	TK	1180A	2150	Derby	8.49	£4673	13.66
D2133	TO	1178A	9517	Derby	3.48	£4753	13.67
D2133	TO	1178A	9518	Derby	12.47	£4752	9.67

Notes:
56104-5 were in the Llandudno-Manchester 'Club' train in 1956.
56200-1 were stored at Craven Arms from 12.46 to 5.48 and then at Derby. They were probably never in service in the UK.
823 was stored at Craven Arms from 3.47 to 5.51, was in the 'North Wales Land Cruise' train in 1953-4 and in North Wales in 1962.

P. Wood, Sheffield: 9006 1.64.
Arnott Young, Troon: 5814 11.64.
Kings of Norwich: 56004-5 9.65; 56303-4 5.65; 823 9.64; 2148 9.68.
Derby: 56100-1 3.64.
Birds, Bynea: 56104-5 6.64; 56502-3 6.64.
Central Wagon Company, Ince: 56302-3 1.66.
Withdrawn after fire damage, Law Junction 13.6.66.

BIBLIOGRAPHY

Books

Allen, Cecil J. *British Pacific Locomotives* Ian Allan 1962
Bishop, Fred C. *Queen Mary of the Iron Road* Jarrolds, 1946
Bond, Roland C. *A Lifetime With Locomotives* Goose & Son, Cambridge, 1975
Carter, Clive S. *LMS-LMR Passenger Train Formations 1923-1983* Ian Allan 1987
Clay, J. F. and Cliffe, J. *The West Coast Pacifics* Ian Allan, Shepperton, 1976
Cox, E. S. *Chronicles of Steam* Ian Allan, Shepperton, 1967
Cox, E. S. *Locomotive Panorama Vol 1* Ian Allan, Shepperton, 1965
Doherty, Douglas *The LMS Duchesses* Model and Allied Publications, Hemel Hempstead, 1973
Jenkinson, D and Essery, R. J. *An Illustrated History* of *LMS Standard Coaches Part 3,* Oxford Publishing Company, Ian Allan, Shepperton, 2000
Jenkinson, D and Essery, R. J. *Locomotive Liveries of the LMS* Roundhouse Books, Ian Allan, 1967
Mullay A. J. *Streamlined Steam, Britain's 1930's Luxury Expresses* David & Charles 1994
Powell, A. J. *Stanier Pacifics at Work* Ian Allan, Shepperton, 1986
Rogers, Colonel H. C. B. *The Last Steam Locomotive Engineer: R. A. Riddles CBE* Allen & Unwin, 1970
Rowledge, J. W. P. *The LMS Pacifics* David & Charles, Newton Abbot, 1987
L. M. Pacifics, a Pictorial Tribute Roundhouse Books, 1967

Journals

British Railways Illustrated Volume 9, April 2000 'Old Plates for New' Michael Brooks
Railway World Volume 40, February 1979 'Naming the First LMS Pacifics' Michael Brooks

INDEX

American Tour
  Tour description 74-8
  Train for 61, 63-4, 67, 69, 70
Authors
  Allen, Cecil J. 27-8
  Beaver, S. H. 33
  Vale, Edmund 39, 46

Belpamela M. S. 74
Boxpok wheels 7

Carriages
  1937 stock 11, 18, 24-5
    Contractors for 18
    Detail description 11, 18
  1939-47 stock 61, 63-4, 67, 69-70, 80, 91
Christen Smith Line 74
Coal consumption 7, 57-8
Coronation of King George V, 1911 5
Coronation of King George VI, 1937 5, 59

Germany 3

Journals
  British Railways Illustrated 98
  Railway Gazette 8
  Railway Magazine 27
  Railway World 98
  Stephenson Locomotive Society Journal 33

Locomotives
  'A4' 7, 31
  'Castle' 3
  'Coronation' 3, 8-11, 40, 87-8
  'George the Fifth' 5-6
  'Hudson' 7
  'Jumbo' 5
  'King' 74
  'Princess Royal' 5-6
  'Royal Scot' 60
Lord Stamp 5, 60, 74, 78

Nameplates 5
Names, 'Coronation' class 6
New York World Fair 60, 74, 78
Nicknames 6

Railways
  Baltimore & Ohio 74, 78
  Chicago, Burlington & Quincy 3
  German State 3
  Great Western Railway 2, 74
  London & North Eastern Railway 1, 3, 59
  London & North Western Railway 5
  Milwaukee Road 3
  New York Central 3, 7
  New York, New Haven and Hartford 77, 79
  Sante Fe 3

Research
  Wind tunnel 6-8, 40

Smoke deflectors 7
Streamlining 1, 3, 81
  Problems with 40, 85-7
  Removal from 'Coronation' class 87-8
  Wind tunnel tests 6-8, 40

Tests
  Test run, Euston-Crewe 27-8, 30
  Wind tunnel 6-8
Trains
  'Cheltenham Flyer' 3
  'Coronation Scot' 3
    American tour 59-68, 74, 78, 80
    High-speed test 27-8, 30
    In service 33
    Plans for 1940 train 91, 93-4
    Publicity for 39
    Train for America 59-61, 63-4, 67, 69-70, 80
    Withdrawal 81
  'Empire State Express' 3
  'Flying Hamburger' 3
  'Hiawatha' 3
  'Lancastrian' 3
  'Mid-Day Scot' 25
  'Royal Scot' 33
  'Silver Jubilee' 3
  'Super Chief' 5
  Test train, Euston-Crewe 27-8, 30
  Test train, Euston-Glasgow 5
  '20th Century Limited' 3

USA 1, 74-8

Plate 139: *Articulated twin RTO/TK Nos. M56302/3M in a Euston-Northampton train in the 1950s.* Paul B. Bromige collection

Plate 140: Coronation *in the shed yard at Polmadie in June 1953, still a magnificent sight but quite different from when it first appeared sixteen years before. It has been specially prepared for working the Royal Train with white lamps on all four lamp-irons and the Scottish royal arms on the front of the smokebox and on the smoke deflectors. In the early morning of 23rd June 1953 the Royal Train was worked by two class '5' 4-6-0s, Nos 45118 and 45481, from Carlisle to Ravelrig Junction, where it was staged for two hours before proceeding to Edinburgh (Princes Street) behind* Coronation. *The engine lost its streamlining in 1946 but still retains its sloping smokebox.*

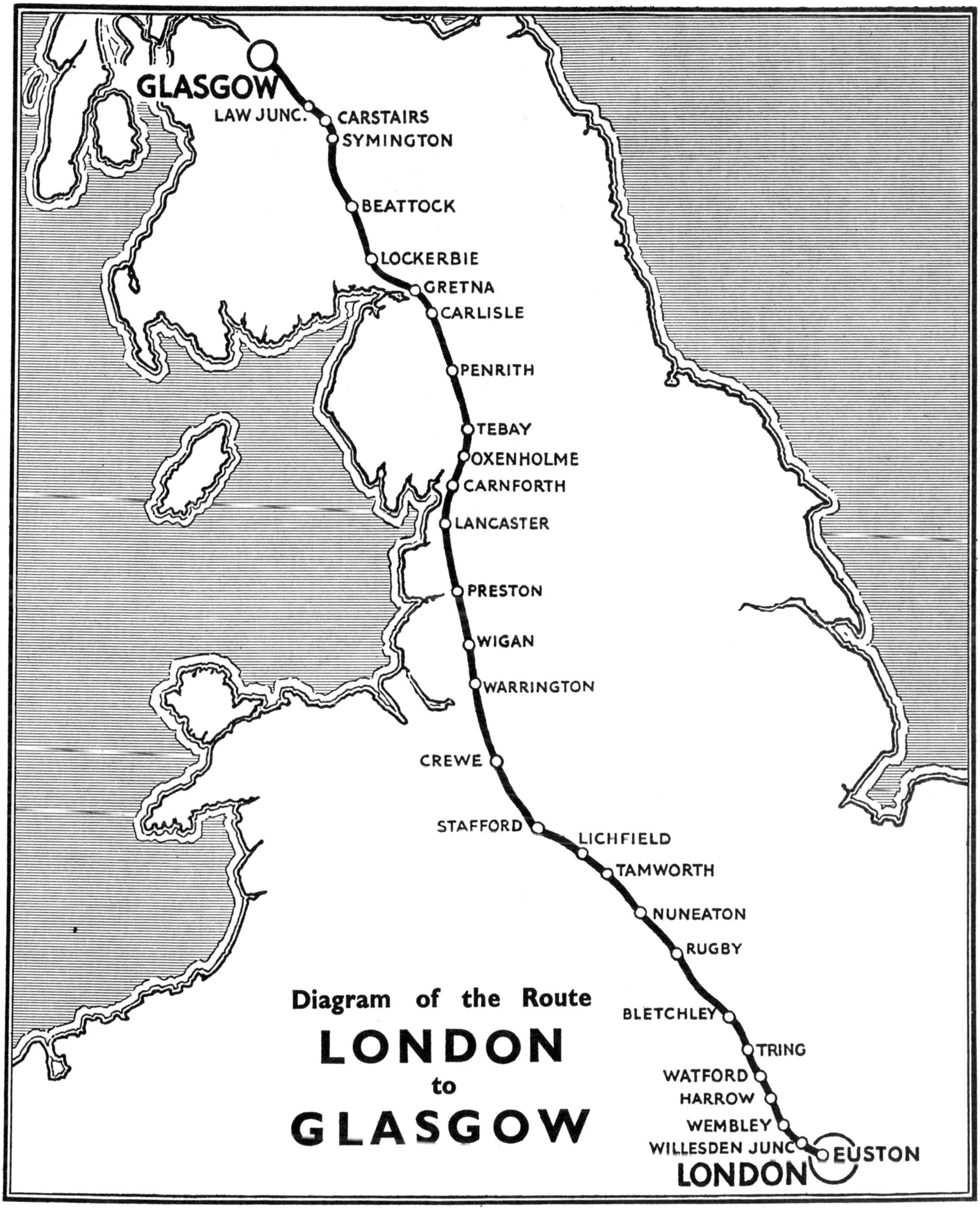

Diagram of the Route

LONDON

to

GLASGOW

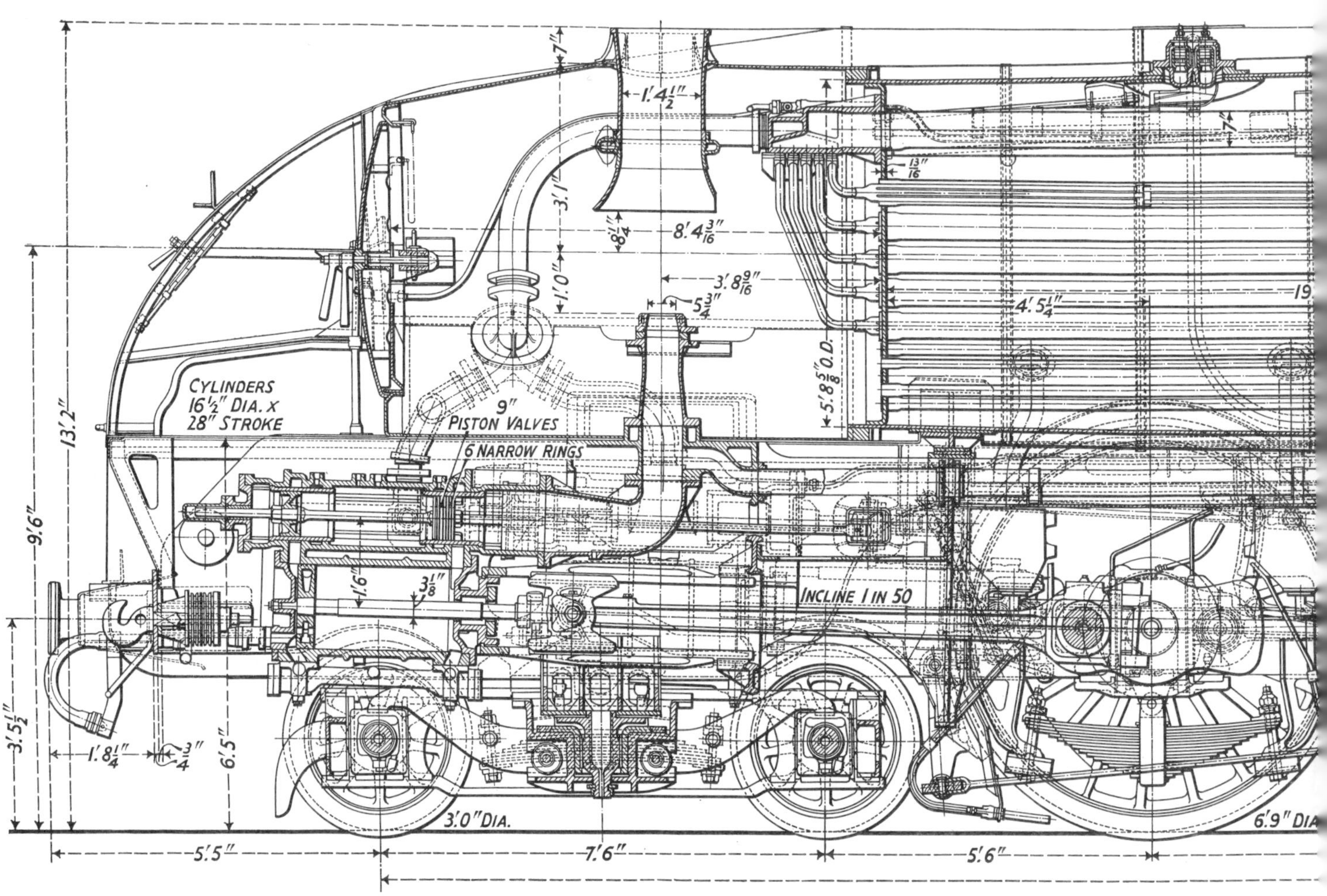

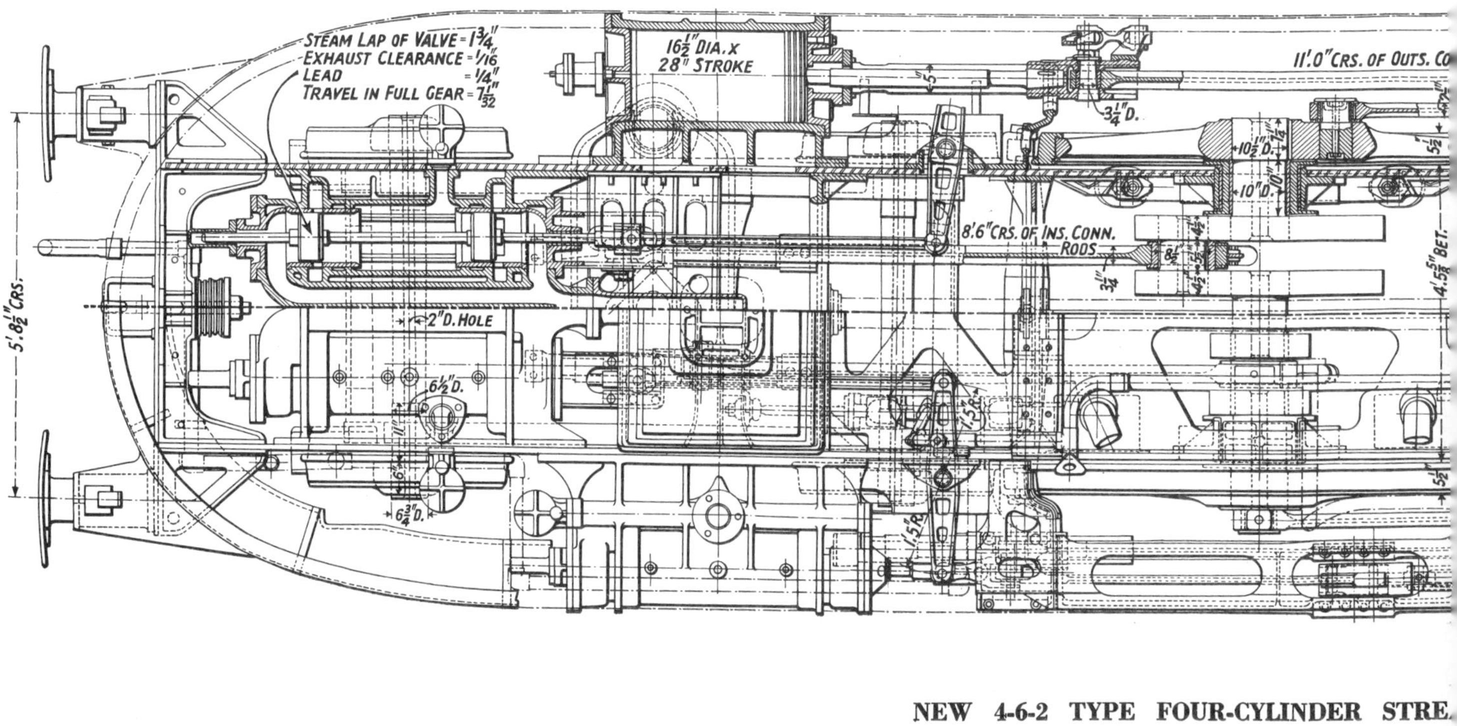

NEW 4-6-2 TYPE FOUR-CYLINDER STRE

Completed at the company's works, Crew